T0078066

# THE FINAL CATCH
## A BIBLICAL GUIDE TO
# SOUL WINNING

**Jeff Bravard**

**BALBOA**.PRESS
A DIVISION OF HAY HOUSE

Copyright © 2021 Jeff Bravard.

All rights reserved. No part of this book may be used or reproduced by any means, graphic, electronic, or mechanical, including photocopying, recording, taping or by any information storage retrieval system without the written permission of the author except in the case of brief quotations embodied in critical articles and reviews.

Balboa Press books may be ordered through booksellers or by contacting:

Balboa Press
A Division of Hay House
1663 Liberty Drive
Bloomington, IN 47403
www.balboapress.com
844-682-1282

Because of the dynamic nature of the Internet, any web addresses or links contained in this book may have changed since publication and may no longer be valid. The views expressed in this work are solely those of the author and do not necessarily reflect the views of the publisher, and the publisher hereby disclaims any responsibility for them.

The author of this book does not dispense medical advice or prescribe the use of any technique as a form of treatment for physical, emotional, or medical problems without the advice of a physician, either directly or indirectly. The intent of the author is only to offer information of a general nature to help you in your quest for emotional and spiritual well-being. In the event you use any of the information in this book for yourself, which is your constitutional right, the author and the publisher assume no responsibility for your actions.

Any people depicted in stock imagery provided by Getty Images are models, and such images are being used for illustrative purposes only.
Certain stock imagery © Getty Images.

Scripture taken from the King James Version of the Bible.

Print information available on the last page.

ISBN: 978-1-9822-6985-2 (sc)
ISBN: 978-1-9822-6984-5 (e)

Balboa Press rev. date: 06/15/2021

# CONTENTS

# CHAPTER 1

# HOW THE DISCIPLES GREW IN THE FAITH

1) They believed

Water turned into wine

**This beginning of miracles did Jesus in Cana of Galilee, and manifested forth his glory and his disciples believed on him (John 2:11)**

Temple cleansing **(Read John 2:17 & 22)**

**But seek ye first the kingdom of God, and his righteousness; and all these things shall be added unto you. (Matt. 6:33 cf. Mark 10:17-31)**

Jesus was teaching them to put God and His kingdom first. The carnal things that seemed so important to these men were a hindrance for them to follow Jesus. They put them first in their life and Jesus was trying to show them that following Him and preaching the gospel was more important.

Solomon taught us in the book of Ecclesiastes that "all is vanity". This world will pass away but God and His kingdom won't. Many people have missed salvation to "whosoever will call upon the name of the Lord". They are not willing to let go of what they have so God can give them what He has, which is eternal life.

1

2) Commitment

**Matthew 4:19-20**

**v.19 And he saith unto them, Follow me, and I will make you fishers of men.**

**v.20 And they STRAIGHTWAY left their nets, and followed him.**

They didn't hesitate to follow Jesus. They immediately left their world behind them, ready to pursue a new one. It is VERY important to have a willing mind and heart to follow Jesus daily. Some people waste time contemplating if they will follow the Lord. There will be a day when their time will be up.

**Seek ye the Lord while he may be found, call ye upon him while he is near. (Isaiah 55:6 cf. Heb. 3:15)**

**And he said to them all, If any man will come after me, let him deny himself, and take up his cross daily, and follow me. (Luke 9:23)**

Jesus said "deny himself" which means that serving the Lord means more to them than their own life. We will be more passionate about serving the Lord and eager to help establish the kingdom of God by spreading the gospel. To do this we must surrender to the lordship of Jesus. We do this by obeying his commandments daily and doing those things that are pleasing in his sight.

**Matthew 16:25-26**
**v.25 For whosoever will save his life shall lose it: and whosoever will lose his life for my sake shall find it.**
**v.26 For what is a man profited, if he shall gain the whole world, and lose his own soul? Or what shall a man give in exchange for his soul?**

"Save his life" by living according to their own purposes and his desires. "Shall lose it" means to miss out on all of the things the Lord offers them who love him. It makes no sense at all to be selfish and live according to our desires. Sinners will only enjoy this world and never enter the joy of the Lord as a believer on Earth or in heaven. Carnal believers who enjoy this world will miss out on what the Lord has for them.

3) They took action

**Matthew 9:18-19**
**v.18 While he spake these things unto them, behold, there came a certain ruler, and worshiped him, saying, My daughter is even now dead: but come and lay thy hand upon her, and she shall live.**
**v.19 And Jesus arose, and followed him, and so did his disciples.**

The disciples followed Jesus to be with him in this time of need. They must have cared about what was happening to get involved the way they did. I am sure the example that Jesus had showed them was a big influence in their life at this time. And even more as they continued to follow him. In Acts, you read time after time where they took action by preaching, casting out devils, miracles, etc. They were putting their faith into action.

**But wilt thou know, O vain man, that faith without works is dead? (James 2:20)**

4) They were willing to learn more

**Then Jesus sent the multitude away, and went into the house: and his disciples came unto him, saying, Declare unto us the parable of the tares of the field. (Matthew 13:36)**

The disciples were willing to learn more. They were always asking Jesus questions about the kingdom of God. The Bible says "Ye have not because ye ask not" refers to prayer. But the disciples proved they were willing to follow Jesus by continually trying to learn more. Each of us needs to continue to strive to learn more about our Lord and the kingdom of God to be fruitful in our salvation.

**More to be desired are they than gold, yea, than much fine gold: sweeter also than honey and the honeycomb. (Psalm 19:10)**

3

5) They were aware of their shortcomings

**Matthew 8:23-27**

**v.23 And when he entered into a ship, his disciples followed him.**

**v.24 And, behold, there arose a great tempest in the sea, insomuch that the ship was covered with the waves: but he was asleep.**

**v.25 And his disciples came to him and awoke him, saying, Lord, save us: we perish.**

**v.26 And he saith unto them, Why are ye fearful, O ye of little faith? Then he arose, and rebuked the winds and the sea: and there was a great calm.**

**v.27 But the men marveled, saying, What manner of man is this, that even the winds and sea obey him!**

I know many believers like to criticize the disciples for being afraid in this passage. I am sure everybody has had some kind of fear in a situation not quite as serious as this one. There are plenty of times when we have fear and we shouldn't because the Master is on board.

**For God hath not given us the spirit of fear; but of power, and of love, and of a sound mind. (2 Tim. 1:7)**

Sound means disciplined or controlled.

6) They didn't judge the sinners

**Luke 5:29-32**
**v.29 And Levi made him a great feast in his own house: and there was a great company of publicans and of others that sat down with them.**

**v.30 But their scribes and Pharisees murmured against his disciples, saying, Why do ye eat and drink with publicans and sinners?**

**v.31 And Jesus answering said unto them, They that are whole need not a physician: but they that are sick.**

**v.32 I came not to call the righteous, but sinners to repentance.**

Jesus and the disciples expressed their love to these sinners by having fellowship with them. They could have got up and left but they stayed with them and accepted them for who they were. They looked beyond their faults and realized these sinners needed salvation. These days Christians might get offended by the very presence of sinners and leave. We should stay and share the gospel and love of God with them. Tell them how much Jesus loves them and present the plan of salvation by telling them about Jesus dying on the Cross for them and raising from the dead.

**Let your light so shine before men, that they may see your good works, and glorify your Father which is in heaven. (Matt. 5:16)**

7) Anointed

**And when he had called unto him his twelve disciples, he gave them power against unclean spirits, to cast them out, and to heal all manner of sickness and all manner of disease. (Matt. 10:1)**

They were anointed for service. Jesus wanted them to prepare the way by sending them to places he hadn't visited yet during his earthly ministry. The disciples were sent to the lost sheep of the house of Israel and instructed to not go unto the Gentiles or into any city of the Samaritans (v.5-6). He wanted them to demonstrate the power of God in the presence of sinners. So they would know that the kingdom of God is among them.

Jesus told them to do four things along with preaching; heal the sick, cleanse the lepers, raise the dead and cast out devils. He went on to tell them, "freely ye have received, freely give". God will anoint Christians for service to bless others and for His glory. It's not for Christians to have show and tell with others. God never intended for us to be selfish with the anointing by keeping it to ourselves. Jesus gave unto others during His ministry by healing, casting out devils, raising the dead, etc. For those who have the anointing, you need to be a blessing to others as much as you can.

8) Served others with humility

**And he commanded the multitude to sit down on the grass, and took the five loaves, and the two fishes, and looking up to heaven, he blessed, and broke, and gave the loaves to his disciples, and the disciples to the multitude. (Matt. 14:19)**

They served others by feeding them fish and bread. We are called to serve others too. Jesus washed the feet of the disciples.

**John 13:14-15**

**v.14 If I then, your Lord and Master, have washed your feet; ye also ought to wash one another's feet.**

**v.15 For I have given you an example, that ye should do as I have done to you.**

**But made himself of no reputation, and took upon him the form of a servant, and was made in the likeness of men. (Phil. 2:7)**

Meekness is not weakness. We need to serve others with humility. Whether we are preaching, teaching or no matter what we are doing. Humility is a very good quality to have. Meekness is a part of the fruit of the Spirit. Meekness will be developed and manifested through us as we walk in the Spirit by dedicating our life to the Lord.

9) Baptism of the Holy Ghost

**And they were all filled with the Holy Ghost, and began to speak with other tongues, as the Spirit gave them utterance. (Acts 2:4)**

They received the power of the Holy Ghost to be a witness and He used them in a mighty way for signs and wonders and other great things. This was the key turning point in their walk with the Lord. Just Compare the disciples before the day of Pentecost to them after they received the baptism, BIG DIFFERENCE.

Jesus needed the baptism too. His ministry started AFTER He received the baptism of the Holy Ghost. That should let us know how important it is for us to receive the baptism of the Holy Ghost, especially if you have a ministry. The anointing is for EVERY believer. If you have accepted Jesus as your Lord and Savior then you are qualified to receive the baptism.

10) Dedication

**And they, continuing daily with one accord in the temple, and breaking bread from house to house, did eat their meat with gladness and singleness of heart. (Acts 2:46)**

It is important to dedicate your life to God and continue daily in prayer, praise and the Word of God. Be faithful in keeping His commandments and going to church every week. (Heb. 10:25) **"The law of the Lord is perfect, converting the soul" (Psalm 19:7)**

**2 Timothy 3:16-17**

**v.16 All Scripture is given by inspiration of God, and is profitable for doctrine, for reproof, for correction, for instruction in righteousness:**

**v.17 That the man of God may be perfect, thoroughly furnished unto all good works.**

**Pray without ceasing. (1 Thess. 5:17)**

**Speaking to yourselves in psalms and hymns and spiritual songs, singing and making melody in your heart to the Lord; (Eph. 5:19)**

# CHAPTER 2

# STUDY THE BIBLE

**Study to show thyself approved unto God, a workman that needeth not to be ashamed, rightly dividing the word of truth. (2 Tim. 2:15 cf. 2 Tim. 3:15-17)**

The early church often disputed about the scriptures over Jesus being the Messiah. Jesus Himself used scriptures to prove who He was. Jesus knew they searched the scriptures and were religious but not righteous. You can study the Bible and learn many truth's about God. But to truly know Him, you must first obey His word and apply it to your daily life. People are easily deceived today because they don't understand the Bible. Many of them don't take time to read or study it.

**The law of the Lord is perfect, converting the soul: the testimony of the Lord is sure, making wise the simple. The statutes of the Lord are right, rejoicing the heart: the commandments of the Lord is pure, enlightening the eyes. (Psalm 19:7-8)**

Millions of Christians are faithful in attending worship services each week. But only a small percentage of them are faithful in reading and studying the Bible during the week.

Notice in **John 16:13** what Jesus says about the Holy Spirit, "he will **guide you into all truth**". The Holy Spirit will guide but we must be willing to follow Him. Christians all over the world should follow the example of those in Berea.

**These were more noble than those in Thessalonica, in that they received the word with all readiness of mind, and searched the Scriptures DAILY, whether those things were so. (Acts 17:11)**

Look at how knowing what the Bible says helped Apollos preach at Ephesus.

**For he MIGHTILY convinced the Jews, and that publicly, showing by the Scriptures that Jesus was Christ. (Acts 18:28)**

If Apollos didn't search the scriptures he wouldn't be able to do this.

CHAPTER 3

# HOW TO PRAY FOR A SINNER ACCORDING TO SCRIPTURE

I want to show you how to pray for sinners according to scripture. This way we can get better results when we pray for sinners to get saved. We won't waste any precious time praying aimless prayers that never accomplish what we want. If you are ever at a shooting range where they have a few different men shooting at the target, you will notice how some are better than others. Some men will hit the target and miss the bull's eye. Then you have those who miss the whole target. From time to time you will find somebody who is really good at this. This man can hit the bull's eye many times because he is very accurate and precise with his approach to the target. This is how we want to pray. We want to be right on target hitting the bull's eye.

1) Prepare their hearts to receive the Word of God

Part of **Matt. 13:23** refer to "the good ground" which is the heart.

Love will melt a person's heart and make it soft. Then the heart will be prepared to receive the Word of God. You don't sow seed on hard, stony ground. You need a soft, tender good ground to produce a harvest.

**Say not ye, There are four months, and then cometh harvest? Behold, I say unto you, Lift up your eyes, and look on the fields; for they are white already to harvest. (John 4:35)**

So when we witness to sinners we have good results with those who have a soft, tender, melted and prepared heart that is ready to receive the Word of God. Love encourages and motivates people to live a better and more fulfilling life. It brings joy, peace, comfort and hope. Hope in believing they can live a good life filled with blessings and the goodness of God.

**Psalm 136** is full of mercy with each verse ending with **"his mercy endureth forever"**. How many times has God shown mercy to sinners and they repented? Mercy can come through several different ways such as forgiveness, food, clothing, shelter and good health.

Healing, deliverance, traveling mercy, protection, a financial blessing, marriage, etc. which often leads to salvation. There have been many times that people got healed and were so thankful and touched by God they gave their heart to Jesus. There were times in the gospels where Jesus would deliver somebody from bondage and they repented and believed in Him. So ask God to prepare their heart through love, mercy and goodness.

2) Lies and deception

**In whom the god of this world hath blinded the minds of them which believe not, lest the light of the glorious gospel of Christ, who is the image of God, should shine unto them. (2 Cor. 4:4)**

**Then said Jesus to those Jews which believed on him, If ye continue in my word, then are ye my disciples indeed; And ye shall know the truth, and the truth shall make you free. (John 8:31-32)**

The only way to counter a lie is by giving them the truth. **Jesus said "Sanctify them through thy truth: thy word is truth". (John 17:17)** Pray for them to receive the truth and be delivered from the stronghold of deception.

3) Understanding

**Then opened he their understanding, that they might understand the Scriptures. (Luke 24:45)**

**"Understanding is a wellspring of life" (Prov. 16:22)**

**"With all thy getting get understanding" (Prov. 4:7)**

**When any one heareth the word of the kingdom, and understandeth it not, then cometh the wicked one, and catcheth away that which was sown in his heart. This is he which received seed by the way side. (Matt. 13:19)**

**Matt. 13:19** makes it clear that the reason the sinner didn't get saved is because they lacked understanding. Satan came when he knew the sinner didn't have understanding and then he came to catch away the word.

**1 Peter 5:8 says, Be sober, be vigilant; because your adversary the devil, as a roaring lion, walketh about, seeking whom he may devour.**

**But the natural man receiveth not the things of the Spirit of God: for they are foolishness unto him: neither can he know them, because they are spiritually discerned. (1 Cor. 2:14)**

Watch what happens when a sinner has understanding and hears the word of the kingdom.

**But he that received seed into the good ground is he that heareth the word, and understandeth it; which also beareth fruit, and bringeth forth, some a hundredfold, some sixty, some thirty. (Matt. 13:23)**

Notice this sinner had understanding and his heart was prepared to receive the Word of God. The verse said "received into the good ground" which is his heart. The sinner who rejected the gospel never had a prepared heart. It makes no mention of it. It says he didn't have any understanding. So the prepared heart comes first then understanding.

Pray for them to have understanding of the Word of God when they receive it. If they don't then they won't get saved. I think this is one of the most important things to pray for when praying for a sinner.

4) Sense of urgency

(Read Jonah chapter 3 for a good example of this.)

**The Lord is not slack concerning his promise, as some men count slackness, but is longsuffering to us – ward, not willing that any should perish, but that all should come to repentance. (2 Peter 3:9)**

**Whereas ye know not what shall be on the morrow. For what is your life? It is even a vapor, that appeareth for a little time, and then vanisheth away. (James 4:14)**

**Boast not thyself of tomorrow; for thou knowest not what a day may bring forth. (Prov. 27:1)**

**Therefore be ye also ready: for in such an hour as ye think not the Son of man cometh. (Matt. 24:44)**

Some people think they have all of the time in the world to repent and get right with God. Any day now the rapture will happen. It could be today, tomorrow, next week, next month or whenever. If we are not right with God when the rapture happens then we will be left behind. We are not promised our next breath. Every day people are taken out of this world when they die. Do you think they planned on dying that day? Each one of us should do some soul searching every day and make sure we are right with God and ready if we die or the rapture happens today. Don't play games with God because you will lose and lose royally! I feel led to warn you that if you are playing around with God and living in sin and refuse to repent. There will be a day that you will be very sorry. Ask yourself where you want to spend eternity.

Pray for sinners to seriously consider where they want to spend eternity and realize that they are not promised their next breath. The next time they go to a funeral they should ask themselves "What if that was me in that coffin"? Or what if the next time they go it is Them. Think about all the people who die each day in a car accident, shot, natural causes at a early age, etc.

5) Grace & faith

**For by grace are ye saved through faith; and that not of yourselves: it is the gift of God. Not of works, lest any man should boast. (Eph. 2:8-9)**

The combination of grace and faith helps leads souls to Christ. Grace is the divine influence upon the heart and it's reflection in the life. **Now faith is the substance of things hoped for, the evidence of things not seen. (Heb. 11:1)** It doesn't matter how good a person is because you can't earn salvation or work your way into heaven.

Pray that sinners will realize it is God's grace to them that allows them the opportunity to get saved **(John 3:16)** and God imparts to us the faith to believe in Jesus when we hear the gospel.

**So then faith cometh by hearing, and hearing by the word of God. (Rom. 10:17)**

6) Work of the Holy Spirit to be completed in the life of every sinner with no hindrances

**And when he is come, he will reprove the world of sin, and of righteousness, and of judgment: Of sin, because they believe not on me; Of righteousness, because I go to my Father, and ye see me no more; Of judgment, because the prince of this world is judged. (John 16:8-11)**

The Holy Spirit does the convicting not us. We witness, the Holy Spirit convicts, draws and deals with the sinners. His work is VERY important in the body of Christ and the world. He deals with sinners to get saved and believers to repent. He empowers and enables us to proclaim the gospel. **(Acts 1:8)** And reveals the truth of the Word of God. **(Luke 4:18-19)**

7) Reveal God to sinners

God reveals Himself to sinners and saints in several different ways.

Moses in the burning bush **(Exodus 3:2)**

Paul on the road to Damascus **(Acts 9:1-19)**

Joseph in a dream **(Gen. 37:5-11)**

Hagar by an angel **(Gen. 16:6-14)**

God spoke to Abraham **(Gen. 12:1-3)**

8) Laws of sowing and reaping

**And herein is that saying true, One soweth, and another reapeth. I sent you to reap that whereon ye bestowed no labor: other men labored, and ye are entered into their labors. (John 4:37-38)**

Pray for sinners who have never received the gospel to hear it today and accept Jesus as their personal Lord and Savior. And for sinners who have already heard the gospel. That God will send a believer into their path to continue to witness to them.

9) God's perfect will to be done in every sinner

**The thief cometh not, but for to steal, and to kill, and to destroy: I am come that they might have life, and that they might have it more abundantly. (John 10:10)**

Jesus loves sinners so much that He not only wants to save them but He wants them to be totally blessed in every area of their life. He cares about ALL of the sinner's life. Whether it be healing, deliverance, or a financial blessing or whatever they need or desire.

10) They must confess Jesus is Lord

**That if you shall confess with your mouth "Jesus is Lord" and shall believe in your heart that God has raised him from the dead, you will be saved. (Rom. 10:9)**

It is not enough to believe in your heart that Jesus is Lord. You must confess with your mouth to receive salvation. Ask and ye shall receive. If they don't ask Jesus to save them and forgive them then He won't. Jesus loves every sinner and wants to save them. He will not force Himself on anybody. They must ask and then He will save them.

**For with the heart man believeth unto righteousness, and with the mouth confession is made unto salvation. (Rom. 10:10)**

# CHAPTER 4

# THE LAWS OF SOWING AND REAPING

## JOHN 4:34-38

**v.34 Jesus saith unto them, My meat is to do the will of him that sent me, and to finish his work.**

**v.35 Say not ye, There are yet four months, then cometh harvest? Behold, I say unto you, Lift up your eyes, and look on the fields; for they are white already to harvest.**

**v.36 And he that reapeth receiveth wages, and gathereth fruit unto life eternal: that both he that soweth and he that reapeth may rejoice together.**

**v.37 And herein is that saying true, One soweth, and another reapeth.**

**v.38 I sent you to reap that whereon ye bestowed no labor: other men labored, and ye are entered into their labors.**

**(For he saith, I have heard thee in a time accepted, and in the day of salvation have I succored thee: behold, now is the accepted time; behold, now is the day of salvation.) (2 Cor. 6:2)**

The laws of sowing and reaping are very interesting when it comes to soul winning. Sometimes God will lead you to witness to a certain person and they give their heart to the Lord. Then there are times it seems like no matter what you say they won't listen to you.

A farmer doesn't expect to reap a harvest until he sows the seed. Then there is a time gap in between sowing and reaping the harvest. **To everything there is a season, and a time to every purpose under the heaven. (Eccl. 3:1)** Sometimes God may use us to sow and other times we are used for the reaping. No matter if you are sowing or reaping you will be rewarded according to your own labor.

First, let's look at sowing which is laying the ground work to reap the harvest. We sow the seed into the sinner's heart by preaching or witnessing to them. **"The seed is the word of God". (Mark 4:11)** The work of the Holy Spirit is the watering process of the seed that is sown and this is how it grows. Then when the sinner is in the presence of the Son it is ready for harvest.

Many times we witness and get frustrated because of the bad results. People aren't accepting Jesus as their Lord and Savior. Sometimes this happens because they aren't ready and God is still dealing with them. Think about it. When you got saved did it take some time for God to deal with you before you gave your heart to the Lord? Don't give up on the sinners who are not accepting Jesus right now. I encourage you to continue to pray for the sinners you have already witnessed to. Then ask God to open the door for you to continue in your efforts of witnessing as the Holy Spirit leads you. If you are sowing then pray for somebody else to reap the harvest of that soul. Or you could ask God for you to reap the harvest.

Then there are times when we are witnessing and people accept Christ. This may be when we are reaping what someone else has sown before us. We have entered into their labor. When you lead a person to Christ make a disciple out of them. By that I mean help them get started in their new life as a Christian. Tell them to start praying, read the Bible and go to church. Encourage them to find a good Bible believing church and go there every week. Tell them when they are praying to just be themselves and talk to God like you would your best friend. Start out reading the Gospel of John and then the rest of the New Testament. Be sure to mention them in your prayers. Ask God to help them grow in the Lord and be strong in the faith. Ask other Christians to pray for them too.

**1 Cor. 3:6-8**

**v.6 I have planted, Apollos watered; but God gave the increase.**

**v.7 So then neither is he that planteth any thing, neither he that watereth; but God that giveth the increase.**

**v.8 Now he that planteth and he that watereth are one: and every man shall receive his own reward according to his own labor.**

I used to be a salesman and we often discussed what is known as the law of averages. This means the more people you talk to the more money in sales you will make. Let's say I am selling coloring books that day. If I wanted to sell 100 of them then it would make sense to talk to at least 100 people that day. It would make even more sense to talk to 200 or more because not everybody is interested in buying a coloring book.

The same thing applies to souls. The more people you talk to the more souls you will lead to Christ. If you want to reap a small harvest then don't witness to very many people. But if you want to reap a great harvest then witness to as many sinners that you possibly can. How big of a harvest do you want? Remember God will reward you for your work.

**For we must all appear before the judgment seat of Christ; that every one may receive the things done in his body, according to that he hath done, whether it be good or bad. (2 Cor. 5:10)**

Do you want Jesus to say, "Well done, thou good and faithful servant"? or "Well"? As if Jesus is saying, "What do you have to say for yourself now"?

# CHAPTER 5

# QUENCH NOT THE SPIRIT

Benny Hinn once said he thought this was the sin of the church. I agree. God sent Jesus to die on the cross for us. Then after Jesus rose from the dead, the Father sent the Holy Spirit so a work could be done in the church. What work? The Great Commission!

**But the Comforter, which is the Holy Ghost, whom the Father will send in my name, he shall teach you all things, and bring all things to your remembrance, whatsoever I have said unto you. (John 14:26) (Read Matt. 28:18-20)**

It would have been a waste of time if Jesus died for us, rose from the dead and ascended into heaven, if nobody would share the gospel of Christ with others. The Father sent the Holy Spirit to help the church because He knew without Him we would fail. If Jesus needed the Holy Spirit then how much more does the body of Christ?

When you read the book of Acts, this was not the Early Church that sat around wasting time doing nothing. You read time after time where the church was busy doing a work for God; preaching, teaching, baptizing, healing, casting out devils, raising the dead, etc. The book of Acts refers to the apostles, the Acts of the Apostles. But notice how they did nothing until the Holy Ghost came upon them. **Acts 1:8 says "You shall receive**

**power AFTER the Holy Ghost is come upon you".** THEN the work of the Holy Spirit was manifested in the disciples.

Quench means to put the fire out. Have you ever felt the unction of the Holy Spirit to say or do something? Then instead of obeying you chose not to do what the Holy Spirit wanted you to say or do. That is an example of quenching the Holy Spirit. The fire was put out on that specific occasion. He wanted to do a work through you to bless another person, group of people or yourself. Notice I said "He" NOT "it". The Holy Spirit is the third person of the Trinity. He did a work in the creation and He will do a work in your life, IF you let Him. Ask God to help you to be obedient to the leading of the Holy Spirit. This will help you draw closer to the Lord and be a better witness.

Sinners won't always listen to us but we must continue to share our faith when we can. If we refuse to do so then we are responsible for that soul. **(Read Ezekiel 3:16-21)** I want to make it very clear that we are responsible for what we do and what we don't do.

**For we must all appear before the judgment seat of Christ; that every one may receive the things done in his body, according to that he hath done, whether it be good or bad. (2 Cor. 5:10)**

**Therefore to him that knoweth to do good and doeth it not to him it is a sin. (James 4:17)**

# CHAPTER 6

# GIFTS OF THE SPIRIT

**"covet earnestly the best gifts" (1 Cor. 12:31)**

What are the best gifts? The gift that is needed at that time is the best gift. If you need healing then prophecy won't help you. Or if you need prophecy then healing won't help you.

**Even so ye, forasmuch as ye are zealous of spiritual gifts, seek that ye may excel to the edifying of the church. (1 Cor. 14:12)**

## WORD OF KNOWLEDGE

**John 4:16-18**

**v.16 Jesus said unto her, Go, call your husband and come here.**

**v.17 The woman answered and said, I have no husband. Jesus said unto her, You have well said, I have no husband:**

**v.18 For you have had five husbands; and he whom you now have is not your husband: in that said you truly.**

These verses clearly reveal that the Holy Spirit was doing a work by manifesting the word of knowledge to Jesus. It revealed facts in the mind of God about a person. The word of knowledge will always reveal facts about the present or past. Now let's look at the result of this gift being manifested.

**v.19 The woman said unto him, Sir, I perceive that you are a prophet.**

**v.25 The woman said unto him, I know that Messias cometh, which is called Christ; when he is come, he will tell us all things.**

**v.26 Jesus said unto her, I that speak to thee am he.**

**v.28 The woman then left her waterpot, and went her way into the city, and saith to the men,**

**v.29 Come, see a man, which told me all things that ever I did: is not this the Christ?**

**v.39 And *MANY* of the Samaritans of that city *BELIEVED ON HIM* for the saying of the woman, which testified, He told me all things that ever I did.**

As a result of the word of knowledge being manifested once, not only did the woman believe in Jesus but she testified and THEN MANY BELIEVED! Oh, it gets even better!

**v.41 And MANY more BELIEVED because of his own word;**

There will be times when you are witnessing and the Holy Spirit will reveal things to you. The three revelation gifts (or gifts that reveal something) are the word of knowledge, word of wisdom and discerning of spirits.

WORD OF KNOWLEDGE AND WORD OF WISDOM WORKING TOGETHER

The word of wisdom is a supernatural revelation about the plans and purposes of God. Wisdom always teaches us how to apply knowledge. Let's look at how these two gifts worked together through Philip the evangelist.

**ACTS 8:26-29**

**v.26 And the angel of the Lord spake unto Philip, saying, Arise, and go toward the south unto the way that goes down from Jerusalem unto Gaza, which is desert.**

**v.27 And he arose and went: and, behold, a man of Ethiopia, a eunuch of great authority under Candace queen of the Ethiopians, who had the charge of all her treasure, and had come to Jerusalem for to worship.**

**v.28 Was returning, and sitting in his chariot read Isaiah the prophet.**

**v.29 Then the Spirit said unto Philip, Go near, and join thyself to this chariot.**

In verse 26, this is a word of wisdom because it deals with the plans and purposes of God for Philip in the present tense. God is all knowing and knew that the eunuch under Candace was passing through. Remember, Jesus saying **"Lift up your eyes, and look on the fields; for they are white already to harvest"?** The Holy Spirit knew the eunuch was searching the scriptures in the book of Isaiah at that time. So He sent Philip to witness to him. In verse 29, the Holy Spirit gave a present tense instruction and the word of knowledge deals with the past or present. Let's see what happened as a result of these two gifts being manifested through Philip.

**v.37 And Philip said, If thou believest with all thine heart, thou mayest. And he answered and said, I believe that Jesus Christ is the Son of God.**

**v.38 And he commanded the chariot to stand still: and they went down into the water, both Philip and the eunuch; and he baptized him.**

DISCERNING OF SPIRITS AND FAITH WORKING TOGETHER

In the next example the discerning of spirits and faith are working together. Discern means to perceive or recognize.

**Luke 8:26-29**

**v.26 And they arrived at the country of the Gadarenes, which is over against Galilee.**

**v.27 And when he went forth to land, there met him out of the city a certain man, which had devils long time, and wore no clothes, neither abode in any house, but in the tombs.**

**v.28 When he saw Jesus, he cried out, and fell down before him, and with a loud voice said, What have I to do with thee, Jesus, thou Son of God most high? I beseech thee, torment me not.**

**v.29 (For he had commanded the unclean spirit to come out of the man. For oftentimes it had caught him: and he was kept bound with chains and in fetters; and he broke the bands, and was driven of the devil into the wilderness.)**

This was obvious that devils were involved and then cast out by faith. Don't expect everybody who has a devil to behave like the man in this passage. Let's see what happened to the man who had the devils called Legion. **(Read Matt. 17:14-21 for a cross reference)**

**v.35 Then they went out to see what was done; and came to Jesus, and found the man, out of whom the devils were departed, sitting at the feet of Jesus, clothed, and in his right mind: and they were afraid.**

**v.36 They also which saw it told them by what means he that was possessed of the devils was healed.**

**v.38 Now the man out of whom the devils were departed besought him that he might be with him: but Jesus sent him away, saying,**

**v.39 Return to thine own house, and show how great things God hath done unto thee. And he went his way and published throughout the whole city how great things Jesus had done unto him.**

Of all the people that were delivered from demonic bondage this is one of my favorites, along with Mary Magdelene. There is no doubt in my mind that he wanted to be with Jesus because He delivered him and Jesus showed him love and mercy.

## GIFTS OF HEALING AND WORKING OF MIRACLES

**ACTS 5:12-16**

**v.12 And by the hands of the apostles were many signs and wonders wrought among the people; (and they were all with one accord in Solomon's porch.**

**v.13 And the rest durst no man join himself to them: but the people magnified them.**

**v.14 And believers were the more added to the Lord, multitudes both of men and women.)**

**v.15 Insomuch that they brought forth the sick into the streets, and laid them on beds and couches, that at the least the shadow of Peter passing by might overshadow some of them.**

**v.16 There came also a multitude out of the cities round about unto Jerusalem, bringing sick folks, and them which were vexed with unclean spirits: and they were healed every one.**

Signs are miracles with an ethical end and purpose. (Lexical Aids) Wonder is an extraordinary thing or act. In this situation, the signs and wonders were an answer to the prayer request by the apostles in **ACTS 4:29-30**

**v.29 And now, Lord, behold their threatenings: and grant unto thy servants, that with all boldness they may speak thy word,**

**v.30 By stretching forth thine hand to *heal* and that *signs* and *wonders* may be done by the name of thy holy child Jesus.**

Verse 14 lets us know that these signs and wonders include healing and miracles led sinners to the Lord because it said "added". In other words, they weren't believers before this happened.

In **Acts 3** we read about the healing of the lame man at the gate of the temple which was called Beautiful. Then Peter preached to the crowd and afterwards Peter and John were brought before the Jewish leaders in **Acts 4.** The healing of the lame man opened the door for Peter to preach. Look at what happened in verse 4.

**Howbeit many of them which heard the word BELIEVED; and the number of the men was about FIVE THOUSAND.**

This is what happened when Jesus performed His first miracle, turning the water into wine.

**This beginning of miracles did Jesus in Cana of Galilee, and manifested forth his glory; and *his disciples believed on him*. (John 2:11)**

**Through many signs and wonders, by the power of the Spirit of God; so that from Jerusalem, and round about unto Illycrium, I have fully preached the gospel of Christ. (Rom. 15:19)**

Jesus brings Lazarus back to life.

**John 11:43-45**

**v.43 And when he thus had spoken, he cried with a loud voice, Lazarus come forth.**

**v.44 And he that was dead came forth, bound hand and foot with graveclothes: and his face was bound about with a napkin. Jesus saith unto them, Loose him, and let him go.**

**v.45 Then *MANY* of the Jews which came to Mary, and had seen the things which Jesus did, *BELIEVED* on him.**

This was the third raising of the dead by Jesus and the most powerful and touching one of them because Jesus wept and MANY JEWS believed in Him. The other two were Jairus' daughter (**Mark 5:21-43**) and the widow's son at Nain (**Luke 7:11-17**).

**Now when he was in Jerusalem at the Passover, in the feast day, MANY BELIEVED in his name, when they saw the miracles which he did. (John 2:23)**

SPEAKING IN TONGUES, INTERPRETATION OF TONGUES AND PROPHECY

**Acts 2:1-8, 12, 41 & 47**

**v.1 And when the day of Pentecost was fully come, they were all with one accord in one place.**

**v.2 And suddenly there came a sound from heaven as of a rushing mighty wind, and it filled all the house where they were sitting.**

**v.3 And there appeared unto them cloven tongues like as of fire, and it sat upon each of them.**

**v.4 And they were all filled with the Holy Ghost, and began to speak with other tongues, as the Spirit gave them utterance.**

**v.5 And there were dwelling at Jerusalem Jews, devout men, out of every nation under heaven.**

**v.6 Now when this was noised abroad, the multitude came together, and were confounded, because that every man heard them speak in his own language.**

**v.7 And they were all amazed and marveled, saying one to another, Behold, are not all these which speak Galilaeans?**

**v.8** And how hear we every man in our own tongue, wherein we were born?

**v.12** And they were all amazed, and were in doubt, saying one to another, What meaneth this?

**v.41** Then they that gladly received his word were baptized: and the same day there were added unto them about three thousand souls.

**v.47** Praising God, and having favor with all the people. And the Lord added to the church daily such as should be saved.

1 Cor. 14:24-25

**v.24** But if all prophesy, and there come in one that believeth not, or one unlearned, he is convinced of all, he is judged of all:

**v.25** And thus are the secrets of his heart made manifest; and so falling down on his face he will worship God, and report that God is in you of a truth.

# CHAPTER 7

# MORE CONVERSIONS!

Jesus at the Feast of Tabernacles (**John 7:25-31**)

Jesus is the True Light (**John 8:28-32**)

Jesus at the Feast of Dedication (**John 10:22-42**)

Chief Rulers Believed (**John 12:42-50**)

Doubting Thomas (**John 20:24-29**)

New Believers in Antioch (**Acts 11:19-21**)

Ministry on Cyprus (**Acts 13:4-12**)

Paul and Barnabas in Iconium (**Acts 14:1**)

Paul and Silas in prison (**Acts 16:16-40**)

Thessalonica (**Acts 17:1-4**)

Berea (**Acts 17:10-12**)

Athens (**Acts 17:16-34**)

Corinth (**Acts 18:1-8**)

Ephesus (**Acts 19:11-20**)

Rome (**Acts 28:16-24**)

CHAPTER 8

# WHY ALL CHRISTIANS NEED THE BAPTISM OF THE HOLY GHOST

———————◦—◦◦—◦———————

**"But ye shall RECEIVE power after that the Holy Ghost is come upon you" (Acts 1:8)**

I put the word receive in caps because it doesn't matter how powerful the anointing is until you receive it. You can read about it, hear about it, talk about it and even witness others who are anointed. But until YOU receive it for yourself, you won't fully understand what it is and how it can change your life.

For those of you who haven't received the baptism of the Holy Ghost yet. I encourage you to pray about it, search the scriptures and seek to be filled. The anointing will help you to have power to be a soul winner for Jesus. Instead of struggling with the flesh you can overcome it by praying in tongues and surrendering to the Holy Spirit by allowing Him to do a work in your life. As you spend more time in the Spirit, you will begin to notice that you have more of a hunger for God than ever before. Then the Holy Spirit will help you to crucify the flesh and your desires will change. Instead of wanting to do earthly things such as sports, hunting & fishing or whatever, you will want to pray, study the Bible, win souls for Jesus and go to church. You will want to do these things more often than before.

Let's look at **2 Corinthians 5:17**:

**Therefore if any man be in Christ, he is a new creature: old things are passed away; behold, ALL THINGS are become NEW.**

Since Jesus came into your heart have "all things" in your life become new? Or are you still holding on to some of those "old things" that should have passed away? Think about it. When you gave your heart to Jesus there were things in your life you knew you needed to repent of. I bet it is safe to say that your life has changed and you repented of SOME things but still struggle with other things in your life. If you have not been baptized in the Holy Ghost then that is what you need to help overcome those "old things" you still struggle with. **(Read Luke 11:13 & 2 Cor. 3:17)**

Let's look at what Jesus told the disciples about the Great Commission in **Mark 16:15-18**

What are we commanded to do?

1) Preach the gospel (v.15)
2) Salvation AND THEN water baptism (v.16)
3) Cast out devils (v.17)
4) Speak with new tongues (v.17) This does NOT mean learn a new language such as Spanish or French or whatever.
5) Take up serpents **(cf. Luke 10:19)** refers to demons NOT actual snakes. (v.18) Some people say that about when the snake bit Paul. Paul didn't take up the snake, the snake came out of the fire and bit him.
6) Lay hands on the sick and they shall recover (v.18)

Jesus never said to stop preaching, baptizing people, lay hands on the sick, casting out devils or speaking in tongues. Show me one verse that says we are commanded to stop doing these things. Some people believe that the apostles took the gifts of the Spirit with them when they died. The Holy Spirit is still here in the world, alive and doing a work in the church.

**1 Cor. 13:8-10**

**v.8 Charity never faileth: but whether there be prophecies, they shall fail; whether there be tongues, they shall cease; whether there be knowledge, it shall vanish away.**

The word "cease" means to pause, to stop. In other words, it still exists but it is temporarily not being used. For example, if I pray in tongues and then stop praying to get something to eat. That doesn't mean that I no longer have that gift. I paused or stopped using it for a short time which can be used again the next time I pray.

In this verse Paul wasn't saying that prophecy and tongues weren't important. He was saying that charity is more important. We have to remember who Paul was writing to, the church at Corinth. These believers were zealous of spiritual gifts but not mature enough to know how to properly use them to bless others. They were selfish and childish. Paul was letting them know that they need to get their priorities in order if they want to be spiritual. Love is far more important than tongues. Even though tongues are also important it should never take the place of loving others.

**v.9 For we know in part, and we prophesy in part.**

**v.10 But when that which is perfect is come, then that which is in part shall be done away.**

In Greek, the word "perfect" means complete. This means the end of the age when Jesus returns. "This gospel shall be preached in all the world THEN shall the end come". (Matt. 24:14) Why? Because the Great Commission is COMPLETE! When the Holy Spirit leaves this world THEN tongues will cease on earth. In order for tongues to be manifested the Holy Spirit must be there to give the utterance. (Read Acts 2:4 & Hebrews 13:8)

Jesus still saves, heals, delivers and baptizes believers in the Holy Ghost today. Every believer who has the gift of speaking in tongues should pray in tongues every day as much as possible. When you pray in tongues you edify yourself (1 Cor. 14:4) and build yourself up on your most holy faith (Jude 20). God is a Spirit and when we pray in tongues, as 1 Cor. 14:14 says "my spirit prayeth".

Praying in tongues will allow you to receive more blessings because you are in the Spirit and you have more faith than before. The Lord can use you to be a blessing to others. Then you will have the opportunity for other gifts of the Spirit to be manifested, instead of only tongues.

Tongues and prophecy is the door through which other gifts often flow. Tongues may lead to prophecy then prophecy will often lead to the revelation gifts: word of wisdom, word of knowledge and discerning of spirits. That is why prophets often begin with prophecy then flow into other gifts or vice versa. In the Old Testament, most prophets were manifesting prophecy, word of wisdom and word of knowledge more than other gifts. That is not to say that other gifts weren't used.

# CHAPTER 9

# REPENTANCE

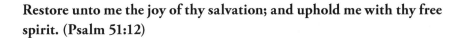

**Restore unto me the joy of thy salvation; and uphold me with thy free spirit. (Psalm 51:12)**

Restore means turn back. David wants to restore his relationship with the Lord. Now we need to keep in mind what events led to this prayer. Nathan had just confronted David for killing Uriah and committing adultery with Bathsheba who was Uriah's wife. David was a man after God's own heart. Even though David made mistakes and sinned he always repented. Not only was he a man of war but he was also a man of prayer. Even as king, David remained humble and close to God.

If you sincerely desire to be a soul winner then you need to have a heart of repentance. In other words, the Holy Spirit wants you to repent when He convicts you of sin and deals with you about other issues. Willingly surrender ALL of your life to the Lord and obey Him DAILY!

Before the Lord will give you a calling to do something for His kingdom. He must first test you and you need to prove yourself to be worthy by earning His trust. You earn His trust by being a spiritual believer that is faithful. Let Jesus be the Lord of your thoughts and desires. THEN the Lord can use YOU for His glory! If you want to be a soul winner then you must understand what happens when someone is converted. (**Read Psalm 51:13**)

Read how God communed with Adam in **Genesis 2** before the fall of man. In chapter 3 God was dealing with Adam about sin, for his disobedience when he and Eve ate of the tree of knowledge. God longs to have fellowship with mankind but sin separated us from God. **(Read Genesis 3:15)**

I love how God immediately put into action the plan of salvation. He was already planning on sending Jesus to save us. Instead of obeying God, Adam was more content in pleasing Eve by taking the fruit. Jesus was the exact opposite. Remember He said **"My meat is to do the will of Him that sent Me, and finish HIS WORK." (John 4:34)**

God was speaking about spiritual conflict between the two seeds. Who are the two seeds? The followers of Satan and the followers of Christ. Christ was to be born of a virgin. Not just any birth but a miracle of God by the Holy Ghost. Jesus was to crush Satan's power and sin by the death on the cross and resurrecting from the grave.

Jesus is the Bridge that allows us to cross over to the other side from death to life so that we are no longer separated from God the Father. God wants to be a part of our life. When we accept Jesus as our personal Lord and Savior, God adopts us into His family and He becomes our Father and we become His children.

As a sinner, the devil was our father. Praise God, we came to our senses and accepted Jesus. Instead of being lost and going to hell with no hope. God intervened on our behalf out of love, mercy and compassion so we could be redeemed by the blood of Jesus.

Without the Holy Spirit none of this would have been possible. The miracle birth was by the Holy Spirit and the ministry of Jesus including the miracles, signs, wonders, healing the sick, casting out devils, causing the blind to see, the lame to walk, the deaf to hear, the dumb to speak and raising the dead. ALL of that was done by the power of the Holy Spirit.

God, Jesus and the Holy Spirit are three separate persons that make up the Trinity. They work together so closely it is amazing to me how they do everything they do. Just think about everything that was said and done, every step Jesus took and every breath He took, He wasn't alone. The only time Jesus was alone was when He was on the cross and cried out, "My God, My God, why hast thou forsaken Me"?

I can't even understand what Jesus must have felt as this happened. The more I think about it, the more I am amazed and deeply touched. It reminds me of the song called "Near the Cross", the part that says "Jesus keep me near the cross". Today, are YOU still near the cross or have you forsaken Jesus?

Just imagine everything God did to have a relationship with you. Take time every day to have fellowship with God. Get alone with Him and pray. Just pour your heart out to Him and don't hold back on anything on your mind and in your heart. **(Read 1 Peter 5:7)**

I want you to think about how much the Lord loves you. How He has changed your life and blessed you. And all of those times the Lord has been there for you when you needed Him. This happens because you have a relationship with Jesus as your Lord and Savior. Now take that same love that you have for Jesus and tell others about Him.

# CHAPTER 10

# WHAT TO SAY TO A SINNER

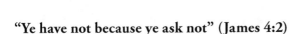

**"Ye have not because ye ask not" (James 4:2)**

It is up to you to talk to the sinner, not the other way around. A good question to ask is "Have you accepted Jesus as your personal Lord and Savior"? This does two things: 1) you are making it clear you are talking about salvation and not religion, joining a church or getting baptized 2) you are asking for a direct response. Ask the Lord to help you to know the right time to witness.

NEVER ask a sinner:

"do you believe in Jesus"?

"do you believe in God"?

"are you a Christian"?

Why? Because they are misleading. **(Read James 2:19)**

Let's face it, these days in America everybody is a Christian. Or at least they claim to be. If you ask "are you a Christian"?, see how many times they respond with "I've been baptized". **(Read Mark 16:16)**

In Greek the word "believe" means to have faith and entrust one's spiritual well being to Christ. Scripture makes it clear salvation comes first THEN water baptism. **(Read John 3:5)** Try to stay focused on Calvary during the discussion, Jesus, the death, burial and resurrection.

Two other questions you can ask:

"Do you believe Jesus is the Son of God"? **(Read 1 John 4:15)**

"Do you believe God raised Jesus from the dead"? **(Read Romans 10:9)**

Some other things you can mention while you are witnessing. Love is one of the things you can talk about. Focus on God's love for the sinner. **(Read Jeremiah 29:11-13)** In those verses it mentions that God has a plan and thoughts of peace toward those He loves. When the sinner gets saved they can have a relationship with the Father, Son and Holy Ghost. God has a plan for everybody. God wants every sinner to repent and accept Jesus as their Lord and Savior. **(Read 2 Peter 3:9).**

Joy is another thing you can talk about. Some sinners think that church is boring and don't want to go. They think being a Christian would be boring so they continue to sin. The Bible says **"the joy of the Lord is your strength" (Neh. 8:10).** Another scripture says **"the pleasures of sin for a season" (Heb. 11:25).** Sinners enjoy sin that is why they continue to sin. Remind the sinner **"the wages of sin is death" (Rom. 6:23)** and they don't have to sin if they don't want to. The Bible says in **Psalms 16:11 "in thy (God's) presence is fullness of joy".** Sinners may think that they are having fun by living in sin but tell them that serving God is fun.

The next thing I want to discuss is peace. **Philippians 4:7 says "And the peace of God, which passeth all understanding, shall keep your hearts and minds through Christ Jesus".** But in the verse before it, it mentions prayer. So if the sinner gets saved then they can pray to God and have peace. I'm not saying they won't have problems or trouble but through prayer they can have peace of mind.

Eternal life can be talked about by telling the sinner about **John 3:16**. Again this mentions love for the sinner. Another scripture you could discuss is **John 10:10 which says "I am come that they might have life and that they might have it more abundantly".**

Jesus came to set the captives free from bondage to sin and Satan. Tell them Jesus not only wants to be their Lord and Savior but also their Deliverer.

Next is hope. Hope is good thing. Jesus offers hope for the sinner. **(Read 2 Cor. 5:17). "For he hath made him to be sin for us, who knew no sin; that we might be made the righteousness of God in him". (2 Cor. 5:21)** Some sinners think they will never be able to change but by the blood of Jesus they can overcome sin by getting saved. The Holy Ghost will help them to repent and the blood of Jesus cleanses us from all unrighteousness.

Last is mercy. God has mercy on all of us. We deserve wrath and judgment but God offers mercy through forgiveness of sins when the sinner accepts Jesus as Lord and Savior. **(Read Psalms 103:12).**

CHAPTER 11

# 16 REASONS WHY SINNERS DON'T GET SAVED

#1 Lack of faith

**Hebrews 3:18-19**
**v.18 And to whom sware He that they should not enter into His rest, but to them that believed not?**
**v.19 So we see that they could not enter in because of their unbelief.**

In verse 18 the phrase "that believed not" in Greek means to go away. In other words, they departed from the faith and fell from grace. God wanted to bless His people with all blessings but He couldn't because of lack of faith. The same thing happens today. **(Read Hebrews 11:6)**

Many Christians don't receive blessings from God such as healing and deliverance because they lack faith in God. If we would pray in tongues and immerse ourselves in the Word of God as much as possible, we would have more faith. Then we would be in the right position to receive more blessings. **(Read Hebrews 11:1)**

In the gospels Jesus often said "thy faith hath made thee whole". If we don't have faith to get the victory then sinners won't listen to us. Sinners want to SEE Jesus not just hear about Him. Do they see Jesus in your life? Try winning souls for Jesus while you are walking around like the devil just beat you up. Stop being defeated and start being victorious. If the world sees us struggling with our faith don't expect the world to run to church searching for answers. The truth is the church hasn't convinced most of the world that Jesus is real. And that is the #1 reason why sinners don't get saved.

#2 Laziness

**That ye be not slothful, but followers of them who through faith and patience inherit the promises. (Hebrews 6:12)**

The passage recorded in **Matthew 26:36-46** where Jesus prays in Gethsemane. The disciples were found sleeping reminds me of the church today...SLEEPING! I can picture Jesus looking at us saying "WAKE UP", saying it with frustration and disappointment.

Now put yourself in Jesus' situation. How would you feel if the people you died for on the cross were doing little or nothing? Think about that for a few minutes. Jesus longs for us to be blessed and be a blessing. **(Read Luke 9:23 & Luke 14:27)**

Jesus wants a church that will make sacrifices to follow Him DAILY. Lazy Christians won't make a sacrifice. How can the Holy Spirit do a work in that kind of Christian? He can't! Then the work of the Holy Spirit is hindered because He needs people who are willing to do a WORK for God, people that He can use for the glory of God. Jesus came To finish the Father's work. The Holy Spirit is doing a work but not all Christians are doing a work for God.

A lazy Christian not only hurts himself but also those who depend on him. If you are a lazy child of God you need to repent! Think of all the sinners who are going to hell that Jesus died on the cross for. They need to hear about His love for them. Some believers never reap a harvest because they are not willing to plant the seed.

**Jesus said "the harvest truly is plenteous, but the LABORERS are FEW" (Matthew 9:37)**

Notice Jesus said "laborers", so it is possible for Christians to be lazy and refuse to work for God. Jesus wasn't saying the church lacked believers. It lacks workers for the kingdom of God. What workers does the Lord want? Those who are willing to obey Him. **(Read 1 Cor. 12:28)**

**Jesus saith unto them, My meat is to do the will of Him that sent Me, and to finish His work. (John 4:34)**

Jesus was saying "This is what I'm concerned with, this is what I care about and this is where My attention is". The reason Jesus said "My meat" is because the disciples were more concerned about food than anything else at the time because of their physical hunger. That is where their attention was. They cared more about food than the kingdom of God at that time. Jesus was teaching them to be willing to do God's will at all times. Even when they are hungry they need to make a sacrifice to be a blessing to other people instead of them thinking about what just matters to them. He wanted them to care about the kingdom of God more than anything else.

**But seek ye first the kingdom of God, and his righteousness; and all these things shall be added unto you. (Matthew 6:33)**

This is a very powerful scripture. Let's take a closer look at what it means. The word "first" means in order of importance. Don't allow people, places, things, etc. to become a hindrance in your walk with God. "His righteousness" is the fruit of the Spirit. "All these things" refer to our daily needs.

When you lack any of "these things" ask yourself, "Have I been putting the kingdom of God and His righteousness first in my life"? The word "and" (before all these things) implies that it is necessary that you obey the first part of that verse in order to receive the last part of it. God's love is unconditional but His promises are not.

#3 Religious NOT Righteous

**Herein is my Father glorified, that you bear MUCH fruit; so shall you be my disciples. (John 15:8)**

The Pharisees in Jesus' day are a good example of some people in the church. They are religious by going through the acts of traditional religion or church. Yet they are NOT righteous by completely surrendering themselves to Jesus by obeying all of His teachings and commandments. Religious people always want righteous people to be silent. **(Read Matthew 23:27-28)**

Imagine being a sinner who has no hope and one day decides to go to church. Instead of finding friendly people who love God, the sinner finds those who are rude and grouchy as if they are mad at the world. Remember **Jesus said "Herein is my Father glorified, that you bear much fruit".** How is the Father glorified in religion? God wants to have a relationship with all of us, especially the sinners. He's not interested in rituals and ceremonies that are meaningless. **(Read Heb. 10:6)** Religious people are a hindrance to the work of the Holy Spirit.

Throughout the Bible you can find many places where people were religious NOT righteous. The same is true today. Millions of people in the world claim to be a part of religion. Religion can't sanctify you, ONLY the blood of Jesus can wash our sins away. **(Read Heb. 9:13-15)**

I know there are people who teach that water baptism is what gets you in to heaven. That is NOT Biblical at all! To teach such a thing is not counting the blood of Jesus as what cleanses us from all unrighteousness and is blasphemy! **(Read 1 John 1:9)** If you go to a church that doesn't believe in the Word of God, I am warning you to get out of there immediately and pray where God wants you to be. **(Read 2 Tim. 4:3-4 and Matt. 13:15)**

Some people are sitting in a church that won't let God do anything. Let me be a little more specific. You have people who are part of the "committee". God has sent preacher after preacher to your church and you keep running them off. If they get excited when they preach, if they preach about repentance, the cross or the blood of Jesus or paying your tithes; the committee will get offended and conspire with others to have that preacher removed. If you have a problem with the preaching of God's Word, then you have a problem with God NOT the preacher!

You even cut down the preaching time to 15-20 minutes so you can have a songfest. Praise has its place but it should NEVER replace preaching. Some of you don't have night services any more. I was told the reason for this is people need more family time. Are you kidding me? These are the same people who never spend time with their family during the week when they have the opportunity to do so. But now that it is Sunday. Suddenly, as if the heavens were opened and the angels and Jesus Himself spoke to them saying "You need to be with your family. You don't have to go to church at night". Here is a crazy idea. Take your family to church and worship together! I have heard of this happening in some churches. **(Read John 3:19-21 and Acts 7:51)**

#4 Lack of Anointing

1)   The Lord has anointed me to preach good tidings unto the meek. **(Read Matt. 11:29 & 1 Peter 3:4)** Both Jesus and Moses shared this quality, they were meek.
2)   He has sent me to bind up the brokenhearted **(Read Isa. 53:3-4)**
3)   To proclaim liberty to the captives

Isaiah was talking about Jesus in these verses. Captive means a prisoner of war. We are in spiritual warfare and Jesus was saying "I know you are in bondage because of sin and Satan. I am coming to set you free. I offer you a spiritual jailbreak".

4)   The opening of the prison to them that are bound

How is Jesus going to set them free? By using the three most powerful weapons He has. (in no particular order) Word of God **(Read Heb. 4:12)**, anointing **(Read Zech. 4:6)**, and His blood **(Read Heb. 9:13-15)**

5)   To proclaim the acceptable year of the Lord and the day of vengeance of our God

In the Old Testament, the Israelites would celebrate the Day of Atonement on the tenth day of the seventh month. This was considered the most important Jewish holy day of the year. The high priest would first offer a bull as a sacrifice for his own sins. Then he would take two goats, one was for the sacrifice and the other was the scapegoat. After he slaughtered the first goat, he took its blood and entered the holy place. He sprinkled the blood on the mercy seat and before the mercy seat. After that, he lays both of his hands on the head of the live goat to confess all the sins of Israel. The goat is sent away into the wilderness which is symbolic of carrying their sins away.

6) To comfort all that mourn
7) To give unto them beauty for ashes
8) The oil of joy for mourning
9) The garment of praise for the spirit of heaviness

Those are the nine things the Lord wants to do with the anointing for His people. Now let's look at the reason He is doing it.

**"that they might be called trees of righteousness, the planting of the Lord, that he might be glorified" (Isaiah 61:3)**

The power of God should NEVER be neglected which is manifested through the gifts of the Spirit. Jesus did miracles and yet the church does not, but we can. **(Read John 14:12)**

#5 Hypocrisy

If you were taken to court for being a Christian would there be enough evidence to convict you? Are we so busy that we can't take time to show the world the love of Jesus? Don't pretend you are an angel on Sunday and then live like a devil the rest of the week. How are you going to win souls for Jesus if you live that way? **(Read Matthew 15:7-9)**

One response I get from sinners when I am witnessing is they don't want to be a hypocrite like so many others in the church. Remind the sinner how much God loves them. He sent Jesus to save them and they can overcome sin by the blood of Jesus and the work of the Holy Spirit. **(Read John 15:5)**

This verse should encourage them and let them know they can serve the Lord with His help. Ask the sinner, "If God went through all that trouble to send Jesus to die on the cross for you. Don't you think God is more than willing to help you serve Him when you accept Jesus as your Lord and Savior? **(Read Romans 8:32, 2 Corinthians 5:17 and John 10:10)**

**2 Corinthians 5:17** is one of my favorite scriptures to use when I am witnessing. Many people reject Christ because they have believed the lies of the devil and the world. They honestly think they aren't good enough or won't be able to repent. The blood of Jesus cleanses them from all unrighteousness. **(Read Jeremiah 29:11, Matthew 7:21-23 and Luke 6:46)**

#6 Lack of effort by the local church

The church doesn't need a "program", they need believers to put their faith into action. Talk is cheap we need action. The book of Acts is about the "acts" of the apostles, NOT what they believed in or talked about. Some believers today will talk to other believers about God but they don't talk to sinners about God. They will get on the phone and talk for hours. I know because I used to do it too. I'm not against Christians having fellowship with each other. But when that is the only thing that you do and never witness, I think you need to repent. **(Read James 1:22 & John 15:14)**

We need more "Paul's" and less "Jonah's" in the church today. Paul was a worker for Christ. Jonah ran from his call. Paul did a great job building up churches. He wasn't a super Christian. He put forth an effort to do something. Paul worked more than the other apostles. The other apostles could have followed his example and build churches everywhere too. Peter and John helped others to get started in their salvation and ministry after they heard what was going on. They did a good work in the early church.

Jesus makes it clear to the disciples there is plenty of work for everybody in the church. God never intended for the preachers to do everything. The congregation needs to get off their blessed assurance and start doing a work for the kingdom of God. **(Read 1 Corinthians 12:12-30)**

#7 Not persistent in witnessing, praying, inviting others to church, etc.

Jesus told the disciples several times there were things that needed to be done daily. Prayer was one of them. Asking is more than just prayer. It can be applied to witnessing and inviting others to church. After we witness we should pray and expect another chance to witness to them again. Or ask God to send somebody else to witness to them. You want to allow the Holy Spirit to be able to work through you. **(Read Matt. 7:7-8 and Gal. 6:9)** When the Lord uses somebody else to witness to the same person you already witnessed to. This is part of the laws of sowing and reaping.

It's important to be persistent in praying for sinners. **Read Luke 18:1-8** about the widow who was persistent. She had a need and never gave up but continued to go to the judge seeking help. The judge wouldn't help her. This is where many Christian's give up and think it is God's will or it would have happened. The enemy fights harder the closer you get to receiving a blessing. DON'T GIVE UP! **(Read Heb. 10:36 & Rom. 8:37)** God wants His people to trust Him and continue asking, seeking and knocking. It is not the will of God for the church to be defeated by the enemy. The church accepts defeat when victory is in sight. In verse 5, the judge decides to help this widow because of her persistence. The judge even admitted it was because of her CONTINUAL coming he gave in. How much more should the saints follow her example?

Be persistent and faithful in witnessing every day as the Lord gives you the opportunity. Ask God to open doors for you to witness and He will do it. Remember, you have not because you ask not. Just like Elijah, you need to listen to that small still voice of the Holy Spirit.

#8 No perseverance

We must be overcomers. If we can't or don't live victoriously then sinners won't be convinced that Jesus is real. **(Read Matt. 16:18-19)** Jesus makes it clear in these verses that He wants us to be victorious over the devil and He gave us the power and authority in His name to do it. No Christian should ever think they can't be strong in the Lord and live victoriously. **(Read Phil. 4:13)**

Our victory was won at Calvary and if we want to receive the fullness of it then we must realize it comes "through Christ" who gives us strength. **(John 14:26)** I asked the Holy Spirit, "What is the most important thing the church needs to remember"? He told me, "The victory that Jesus won on the cross. Too many are defeated because they don't remember and walk in what was given to them".

As a Christian sin, sickness and bondage has no power over you. So refuse to accept it in your life. I'm not saying you won't have problems in these areas. I am telling you that you don't have to ACCEPT those problems. They are NOT from God so refuse to accept it.

Jesus gave you victory!

Redeemer, so that you would be set free from the power of sin.

Healer, so you would be set free from the power of sickness and disease.

Deliverer, to be set free from every kind of bondage.

Provider, so all your needs are taken care of.

Shield, always protected. **(Read Isaiah 53 & 61)**

It doesn't come from man or woman, the preacher, teacher or prophet, ALWAYS through Christ. NEVER on our own strength, wisdom or talent. **(Read Prov. 18:21)**

Too many Christians live in defeat to the enemy (flesh, world and devil) because of our own words. Let me give you an example. Recently, I hurt my hip and I kept talking about how it hurt me. I asked the church to pray for me and nothing happened. I was still in pain. I continued a few more days saying "I'm in pain". Then the Lord reminded me of Proverbs says **"Death and life are in the power of the tongue"**. That is when I changed my speech to "I'm feeling better". Then a couple of days later I was totally healed, no more pain. Glory to Jesus for healing me! What I should have said before I was healed was "Thank you, Lord for healing me. By Your stripes I am healed". At the end of **Isaiah 53:5** it says **"with his stripes we ARE** (present tense) **healed".** We serve a God of the now, His name is I AM.

I was binding myself with my own words. If you are sick or in pain then speak words of life. Use the example I just gave you. God is no respecter of persons. If He healed me then He wants to heal you too. Start praising God for victory BEFORE you receive it. Praise is the language of faith. This works in every area of your life not just healing. Claim victory in your marriage, finances, health, etc. Whatever you need in your life continue to have faith and be blessed. **Study Mark 11:24 "Whatever you DESIRE, when you pray, believe that you receive them, and you shall have them".** Maybe you get depressed and need joy. Count your blessings and praise the Lord. Sing along with gospel music. **(Read Eph. 5:19-20)**

Many Christians are too busy worrying about their problems during church for God to bless them. During the sermon they are thinking about their problems instead of listening so they can be edified. **(Read Rom. 10:17)** How will you have faith if you aren't listening? Jesus healed people and often said, **"Thy faith hath made thee whole".** We all need faith to be blessed and be strong in the Lord. **(Read Heb. 12:1)**

Be victorious and full of joy. Some Christians walk around with their head down, and look depressed. Don't give the devil the satisfaction of you being down. Hold your head up, smile and spread joy to others. Let's look at how to be victorious in our thoughts. **(Read 2 Cor. 10:3-6)** Notice the phrase "pulling down of strong holds". These strong holds are the works of the flesh and demons. **(Read Eph. 6:10-18 & Matt. 5:19)**

The words "high thing" and "itself" make it clear that a demon is active. Also, notice the word "against". Satan and his devils are always against God, His kingdom and His people. Our response to these thoughts should be "revenge all disobedience".

Then Paul goes on to let us know when to do this, "when your obedience is fulfilled". How is your obedience fulfilled? **(Read Gal. 5:16)** Devote your time to prayer, Bible study, praise, worship, soul winning, go to church, etc.

#9 Give up too easy

One person rejects the Lord and we don't bother witnessing to others or invite them to church. I think there are Christians who would rather make excuses about why they don't do anything for the kingdom of God. Instead of continuing to pray for sinners, witness to them and do whatever needs to be done in the church. I heard people say they would never invite anybody to church ever again because they tell you they will be there and then they never show up.

How do you think Jesus feels when He asks us to do something and we don't obey Him? He doesn't just ask once, He keeps on asking until we repent. **(Read Rev. 3:20)** Christians who give up in witnessing and inviting people to church are probably the same ones who never get blessed because they give up on God in answering their prayers. They will say, "It must not be God's will because nothing happened". The Lord told me that some people go all week and don't spend any time with Him at all. Then on Sunday they go to church and act like the Lord is going to open the windows of heaven so that person can receive a blessing.

We need to learn that God does things in His time not ours. Just because we don't receive an answer to our prayer that day, doesn't mean that God won't answer it. Sometimes God's answer to a prayer isn't no, it is not now. **(Read Heb. 6:12)**

Many disciples desert Jesus **(Read John 6:60-71)**. This is a good example of people who give up too easy. Jesus says something they don't understand or maybe refuse to surrender their entire life to follow Him. Backsliders fell from grace because they gave up too easy. Now you think about it. Is a Christian who gives up all of the time an effective witness? **(Read Matt. 24:13)**

Jesus doesn't give up on us when we fail Him. Think about all the times Jesus would call people to do a work for Him and they don't do it. We must realize that the Father's will is more important than we can understand. And it is more important than our own will. **(Read John 4:34)** The church can't leave any work unfinished. Notice Jesus said "His work" referring to God the Father.

#10 Carnal instead of spiritual

Worldly entertainment is a spiritual disease. It enters the church and many embrace it. Worship services have turned into nothing but entertainment. **1 Cor. 14:26 teaches us "Let ALL things be done unto edifying".** That verse refers to church services. Christians who don't pray or read the Bible very often are carnal. Spiritual believers are more interested in seeking the kingdom of God. You can tell if a believer is carnal or spiritual by judging the fruit in their life. Is it more focused on God or the world? If we as believers don't live different than the world why should they repent? We haven't convinced them that God is among us. **(Read Gal. 5:16-18)**

Spiritual believers are the ones who abide in Jesus and bear fruit. Carnal believers do not. These are saints who have accepted Jesus as their Savior but not as their Lord. If Jesus truly was their Lord then they would dedicate their lives to Him by reading the Bible, praying, praising Him and witnessing. They need to repent of sin and turn away from the ways of the world which they have embraced and coveted. Jesus said **"without me you can do nothing".**

The fruit that we bear is not our fruit. It is the fruit of the Spirit being manifested in our life. **Gal. 5:22 say "the fruit of the Spirit"** (Holy Spirit). Fruit refers to character and the nature of a person. If our life is lacking any of the fruit of the Spirit then we must draw closer to God in obedience. And pray that God will help us overcome the flesh. It is "fruit" not "fruits". They are nine clusters that complete one fruit or the fruit. **(Read Luke 9:23)**

Apostle Paul discusses carnal believers throughout **1 & 2 Corinthians.** The Corinthians were living like the world instead of being spiritual in their practical matters. This is the same church Paul told **"be ye not unequally yoked together with unbelievers". (2 Cor. 6:14)**

Carnal believers are in danger of departing from the faith.

**1 Peter 5:8-9**

**v.8 Be sober, be vigilant; because your adversary the devil, as a roaring lion, walketh about, seeking whom he may devour:**

Who will the devil devour?

**v.9 "Whom resist STEADFAST in the faith"**

Steadfast means continuously.

These are the people the devil wants to devour. Now we know "who" he wants to devour but "what" about the person does he want to devour? The Word of God! Compare this to the Parable of the Sower in **Mark 4:13-20.**

#11 Lack of spiritual leadership

Of all the reasons that sinner's don't get saved this one bothers me the most. God put certain people in the church to be a leader. Yet some of them aren't doing a very good job of leadership. I don't understand how these leaders in the church even sleep at night. They are called to lead the church in the faith. They are called to preach the gospel and reach the lost but they don't do it. These people will have to give an account for themselves when they stand in front of Jesus at the Judgment Seat of Christ. **(Read Matthew 9:36)**

In **John 10** Jesus is called the Good Shepherd. This is one of my personal favorite chapters in the Bible. True pastors care for their flock with loving kindness. False pastors are only concerned about themselves instead of the flock. Jesus' love for us is astonishing. He laid down His life for us and that is what separates Jesus from all of the other shepherds.

The purpose of spiritual leadership.

Preachers who follow after Jesus' example of loving and taking care of the congregation are true spiritual leaders. Pastors who are preaching and teaching them the full gospel are obedient servants. True spiritual leaders serve others and don't seek to be served. **(Read Eph. 4:11-13)** A good example is Jesus washing the disciples' feet in **John 13:1-20.**

Not so spiritual leaders.

Some preachers think the pulpit is intended for a comedy show. They spend more time telling jokes and less time preaching. A sense of humor has its place but be spiritual NOT carnal. God is not pleased with preachers who turn church services into a circus. We need to EDIFY not entertain. Some preachers spend more time sharing their opinions and not enough time preaching the Word of God. This is lack of spiritual leadership.

**Ephesians 4:29-30**

**v.29 Let no corrupt communication proceed out of your mouth, but that which is good to the use of edifying, that it may minister grace unto the hearers.**

Corrupt means rotten i.e. worthless.

**Jesus said "But I say unto you, that EVERY IDLE WORD that men shall speak, they shall give account thereof in the day of judgment". (Matthew 12:36)**

Idle also means worthless. Look at the next verse and see how the Holy Spirit feels about all of this.

**v.30 And GRIEVE not the holy Spirit of God, whereby you are sealed unto the day of redemption.**

I must warn you that if you are bringing witchcraft into your church you need to repent of this evil or face judgment. God knows who is doing it. He judged Eli in the Old Testament and Ananias & Sapphira in the New Testament. **(Read Acts 20:28-30)**

It is very important to know what church God wants you in. Not everybody is preaching and teaching the truth of God's Word these days. Ask God to put you where He wants you. I pray that God will expose all men and women who are trying to deceive the Body of Christ.

The Bible mentions there will be a great falling away in the last days. I believe it is already happening and will continue to get worse as time goes on. Jesus warned us that not everyone who says **"Lord, Lord shall enter into the kingdom of heaven but he that does the will of my Father which is in heaven". (Matthew 7:21)**

Do you go to a church that does the will of God or not? If not, then you must ask yourself, "Is it because of lack of spiritual leadership or lack of effort by the congregation"? Please don't think that just because you have a big crowd you are spiritual. What happens when you come together for a worship service? Did anybody get saved? Healed? Delivered from demons? Baptized in the Holy Ghost? Etc. This is something you need to think about. If all you get out of the service is shouting and jumping up and down then that is just entertainment. In the Old Testament false prophets deceived Israel. Deception in the church today is very common.

I sense in my spirit to warn you to be careful of who you listen to preaching, teaching and prophesying. Whether it be in person, or the radio, TV or internet. If you are not careful you could be led astray by believing a lie. Here is what Jesus warned us about in the last days.

**And MANY false prophets shall rise, and shall DECEIVE MANY! (Matthew 24:11) You need to know what the Word of God says. (Read Matt. 7:15, 2 Peter 2 & 1 John 4:1-3 for more about this.)**

**Look at how people are deceived:**

**"come in my name saying, I am Christ" (Matt. 24:5) v.4 too**

**"shall show great signs and wonders" (Matt. 24:24)**

**"by good words and fair speeches" (Rom. 16:17-18)**

**"with every wind of doctrine & cunning craftiness" (Eph. 4:14)**

**"with vain words"** (Eph. 5:6)

**"by any means"** (2 Thess. 2:3)

**"with all power and signs and lying wonders and with all deceivableness of unrighteousness"** (2 Thess. 2:9-10) (Read verses 11-12)

**"having a form of godliness but denying the power thereof"** (2 Tim. 3:5)

**"they will not endure sound doctrine"** (2 Tim. 4:3)

**"they shall turn away their ears from the truth"** (2 Tim. 4:4)

**"who confess not that Jesus Christ is come in the flesh"** (2 John 1:7, 1 John 4:1 & Col. 2:8, 2 Tim. 3:13)

Jesus warns 4 times in Matthew 24 about being deceived. Always pray about who God wants you to listen to and who to avoid. This includes your own family, friends, neighbors, co-workers, etc. who to avoid. I'm not saying be paranoid but pray about who you socialize with. Who you invite into your home, eat with and who your children and grandchildren should avoid.

Joshua is an example of a true spiritual leader **"as for me and my house, we will serve the Lord".** (Joshua 24:15)

Joshua is very bold speaking to a disobedient people, the Israelites. Notice he said "we" not just him but his entire house. True men and women of God who desire to be a leader in the church must first learn to be a leader of their own house. **1 Timothy 3** is a good chapter to read about who qualifies to be a spiritual leader.

Lack of support.

Congregations all over the world need to support their pastor and other leaders in the church. Pray for them daily and give them words of encouragement as the Lord leads. Some people would rather give up on a preacher when he or she has trouble in their walk with God. Preachers aren't perfect they are tempted too. I wonder how many prayers went up for those preachers who fell from grace. I know the Bible says **"work out your own salvation"**. But the church needs to stand by their pastor and pray for God's perfect will to be done.

Body Ministry

In **1 Cor. 12:12-31** Paul is talking about how the church is one body but many members. This is a good passage to read about the congregation working together instead of the preacher doing all of the work. Some people think you can know how spiritual a pastor is by knowing how spiritual the congregation is. This isn't always true. Look at Moses being a leader of Israel. They were a disobedient nation but Moses was very close to God.

Failure to preach the truth

There are people who are going to church thinking they are a Christian. The truth is they are lost in sin because they haven't accepted Jesus as their Lord and Savior. Jesus said "You must be born again". These people have never been born again. And you are born again ONCE not over and over. I asked somebody "Are you born again"? He said "Oh yes, I have been born again three times". I told him Jesus said to be born again not born again, again and again.

The story of the Prodigal Son refers to two sinners. The one who left was the backslider. And the one who stayed in the father's house is a lost church goer. He stayed in the father's house but didn't realize that he was lost. I will be discussing this more in the chapter called The Lost Church Member. **(Read John 8:31-32)**

Anointing

Every church leader needs the anointing. When you have the anointing in your church, more souls will get saved. Stop trying to win a spiritual battle in the flesh. You need to receive the anointing. Then the Holy Spirit can do a work in your church.

If you don't think you need the anointing. I want you to compare the disciples before they received the anointing to what happened after they received the anointing. Peter preached two sermons in the beginning of Acts and about 8,000 souls were saved. This happened WHEN Peter was anointed. This is the same man that denied his Lord not long before this. Receive the anointing and believe God for miracles!

#12 Disobedience to the Great Commission

Every church NEEDS an outreach ministry. I encourage you to reach the lost in your community and get the whole church involved. **(Read Matt. 28:18-20 and Mark 16:15)**

The Apostle Paul visited many places on his missionary journeys. He helped establish several churches throughout the then known world. Paul knew that the Great Commission was the backbone of the Body of Christ. He preached the gospel in the power of the Holy Ghost.

Paul would visit these churches to see if they were growing in the faith. He truly set the example of how we should take care of churches. Also, he wrote letters to teach and admonish them how to be more spiritual and give them encouragement. Sometimes Paul had to give them discipline. Just like a father protects his children Paul was protecting the saints. I think the most common mission field that is overlooked is our own backyard. We tell everybody else about Jesus except our own family and community.

*The Lord gave me a vision. I saw a busy street with people walking up and down the sidewalks. They are crying out to Jesus. Not with their mouth but from their inner man. They are crying out "Where can I find Jesus"? They looked to the cross, it was empty. They looked to the tomb, it was empty. They went to church, but all they found was entertainment. So they got up, left and never came back. They are still in the world today crying out "Where can I find Jesus"?*

*Then suddenly Jesus began to cry out saying "Why won't the church take the gospel to these sinners who keep crying out to Me everyday"? Then Jesus said "Tell the church if they want revival to go to the streets and they will find it there".*

#13 Robbing God in tithes and offerings

There is a lack of finances to spread the gospel. **(Read Malachi 3:8)**

Financial support is a BIG part or role in spreading the gospel all over the world. Don't believe the lie that God doesn't want your money. God needs believers to help pay for the costs of the Great Commission. It takes money to build churches, buy the materials, supplies, songbooks, Bibles, etc. These are things that should never be neglected.

It is a terrible thing for a missionary to be sent home due to lack of financial support. God calls men and women to spread the gospel to foreign countries. These foreigners are lost in sin and need Jesus. The Lord loves them and wants to be their God. Imagine them not being able to hear the gospel because the church doesn't support missions enough financially. What do you think Jesus will say to us? **(Read Rom. 10:14-15)**

Think about all of the money that we throw away on things that we don't need. Everyday the church wastes MILLIONS of dollars that could be used to help spread the gospel of Jesus Christ. To tell people that Jesus loves them and share with them the plan of salvation by preaching the cross and resurrection. And letting them know that the blood of Jesus washes their sins away when they accept Him as their Lord and Savior. Think of what would happen if every Christian would set aside $1 per day for the sole purpose of spreading the gospel all over the world. (Plus, your tithes)

You know I don't think the church understands how important it is to pay their tithes and offerings. The tithe is 10% of your income and the offering is anything above and beyond that. Some people say "I'm not giving God any of MY money". The tithe belongs to God and if you give Him the tithe you are returning His property.

*Jeff Bravard*

I always think its good when a missionary does a work for God and is blessed. I often enjoy hearing about how they are a blessing to others. People who spread the gospel all over the world are doing a wonderful work for the kingdom of God. It would be a terrible thing if one day these ministries could no longer spread the gospel due to lack of financial support. We should all pray about who God wants us to support financially. It could be a ministry or local church, etc. I believe the tithe goes where you are blessed each week. If you attend a church then give them the tithe. If you are unable to attend church services and watch Christian TV then support them. **(Read 2 Cor. 9:6-7)** If you don't give money for the gospel then you are actually robbing Jesus of glory He could be receiving. If you love Jesus then be a giver and pray about who to support and how much to give. God wants us to be wise stewards with our money. Don't just give to anybody ALWAYS pray about it!!! (I can't stress that enough.)

#14 Spiritually dead church services

**1 Cor. 14** is a good example of how a church service should take place. **(Read 1 Cor. 14:22-33)**

A spiritually dead church service is one where the work of the Holy Spirit is not being manifested. Whether it be the gifts of the Spirit or whatever. The Holy Spirit will draw people to Jesus and deal with them by convicting them of sin. He will also move upon a person to say or do something during the service. And give them specific details of what needs to be said or done.

Every part of the worship service should be prayed for. What I mean is the Sunday school teacher should seek guidance from the Lord in prayer on how to teach the lesson each week. The song leader should pray about what songs or choruses to sing. If somebody is going to sing a solo they need to pray about that too. When the usher takes up the offering, be led by the Holy Spirit on how to pray over the offering. The preacher should pray about what sermon to preach and listen to the Holy Spirit while preparing and preaching the message. Listen to that still small voice. Many times the Holy Spirit will inspire the preacher to use certain scriptures for the sermon.

Never neglect the altar service because it is very important. This is where many people get blessed. Whether it is salvation, healing, deliverance or being baptized in the Holy Spirit this is a good time for the gifts of the Spirit to be manifested and change lives.

My life was changed by going to the altar because that is where I got saved. When I decided to go to the altar, I stood up and then I had a vision of Jesus. He was standing in front of the Lamb's Book of Life. Jesus told me "Jeff, I'm writing your name in the Lamb's Book of Life". Then I saw Him begin to write and the vision ended. You have to know that I never even knew there was a Book of Life.

Now let me share with you the flip side of the altar service. What if you don't obey the Lord by not going to the altar? Many people, including myself, have missed out on what God has for them because they don't obey His voice. When He tells you to go to the altar during the altar service don't waste any time, GO! I don't know if it's confusion, fear, unbelief or what that prevents people from going to the altar.

Some people feel like they aren't worthy or good enough to be blessed because all they have ever known in their life is rejection. Don't ever let the devil rob you of a blessing. I want you to always remember this. JESUS LOVES YOU! You are precious in His sight. He wants you to be blessed in every part of your life. Don't ever think you are not worthy. God wants to see you full of joy not being depressed and down trodden.

If you don't go you will miss out on the blessing God has for you. He knows what you need before you even pray about it. He understands your fears and weaknesses too. Put your trust in Him and He WILL bless you.

#15 Lack of prayer to support those who are spreading the gospel

**I thank my God, making mention of thee always in my prayers. (Philemon v.4) (Read 2 Thess. 3:1-2)**

In **Acts 12:1-19,** read how Peter was delivered from prison when believers prayed for him. Peter was a good man of God and he even needed prayer. **(Read 2 Peter 2:4 & Luke 22:31-32)**

Paul asked for prayer more than the others. He knew the importance of intercession and wanted as much help as possible. Paul understood that even though he was a spiritual leader he isn't perfect and needs God to help him. Intercession may be defined as persevering prayer when somebody pleads with God on behalf of others.

#16 Judging

I can't tell you how many times I have heard people say "You are not supposed to judge others". This usually happens when I rebuke someone about sin. Nobody likes to be told they are doing something they shouldn't be doing. Jesus was talking about religious people who would condemn others for being poor or whatever. **(Read Romans 2:1-4 cf. Matt. 7:1-6)**

Today in the church it still happens. How many times has a sinner come to church and was turned away for not being dressed a certain way or whatever the reason may be? I wouldn't want their blood on my hands when I stand before the Lord. Jesus died on the cross for the sinner not the righteous. He came to seek and save the lost. **(Read Romans 10:13)**

If you are turning people away from God you need to repent. This is a very evil thing in the sight of God. Don't turn them away because they are poor, not properly dressed, they have bad hygiene, gay or lesbian, hooked on drugs or alcohol, witchcraft, the way they look or any reason at all. If Jesus wouldn't turn them away then why are you doing it? You need to obey the commandments of God instead of trying to enforce the commandments made up by men.

How about past sins or grudges? Maybe it is a brother or sister in Christ that you have a problem with. Instead of helping them to grow in the Lord you keep bringing up the past. Christians fighting each other is a good way to keep sinners from getting saved. Have you ever heard a sinner say "Well, if that is a Christian then I don't want to be one"? The Body of Christ must repent of this childish and selfish behavior. **(Read John 7:24)**

# CHAPTER 12

# DON'T WASTE TIME

Most Christians are living as if they have all of the time in the world to tell people about Jesus, including their own loved ones. **(Read Proverbs 27:1)** JESUS IS COMING VERY SOON! People need to get ready for His return. Sinners don't have very much time to get saved. It is up to us to take the gospel to a world of lost souls who need Jesus in a desperate way. **(Read Matthew 24:36-44)**

Some believers are not taking this very seriously. If you are right with God then you are safe. What about all those sinners we keep saying we will witness to but haven't done it yet? Will we wait until they die and then say "I knew I should have told that person about Jesus when I had the time to do it"? This is not a game. You can't start over and try again. When a sinner goes to hell there is nothing we can do for them. Then it's too late to do anything. NOW is the time to reach them with the gospel of Jesus Christ before it is too late.

I want you to be honest with yourself about something. During the last week how many sinners did you talk to about Jesus? Was there a time when the Holy Spirit was dealing with you to witness to a sinner and you didn't do it? We walk right by people every day and we don't take the time to tell them about Jesus. I guess we think somebody else should do it even when we have the opportunity to do it. If the whole church thinks that way then guess who does the witnessing? NOBODY! **(Read Matthew 25:32-33)**

I want you to imagine standing there on that day, Judgment Day. When we are looking around to see who made it and who didn't make it. As you are looking around at the sinner's maybe you recognize some of them. Then you remember how you could have witnessed to them but for whatever reason you chose not to do it.

Then instead of just noticing those you saw in public. Then you see your friends that you talked to about all kinds of things. Just like all friendships you were close and would share anything with each other. Then you remember, "I never told them about Jesus".

Finally, you see your family and you are devastated, shocked and amazed that they didn't make it. You prayed that somebody would witness to them because you love them and want them to go to heaven. As you think about all of the times you were together. You can't believe it, that you never took the time to witness to your own family. And you had many, many chances to do it.

You spend those final moments looking at them. Maybe even crying out "I'm sorry that I never told you that Jesus loves you and He wants to save you. And have a relationship with you". Then as you are separated it sinks in that there is nothing that you can do to change anything. They are separated from you forever. They are gone. **(Read Matthew 25:46 and James 4:4)**

CHAPTER 13

# BE A GOOD LISTENER

Some Christians aren't very good listeners. You tell them something and they don't pay attention to you. I am sure you have talked to somebody and you knew they weren't listening to you. Then the next time they come around you might not be so eager to talk to them. Of course, we can't forget about the ones who never stop talking. I bet they talk in their sleep. You know the ones that I am talking about because you try to avoid them as much as possible.

How about in our prayers? We do all of the talking and never let God say anything. That reminds me of when I was praying and the Lord said "Can I get a few words in"? I know we have needs to tell the Lord about when we pray. We should just learn to be silent and wait on Him. It will really help us to grow in the Lord. He may tell us something to bless us. All we have to do is take time to listen.

Some couples say they don't ignore each other, they have selective hearing. How many times has your spouse sent you to the store and you didn't pick up everything you needed because you weren't listening? We miss out on so many things when we don't listen. **(Read Acts 8:29)**

If Philip wasn't listening then he would have missed this opportunity to witness. As a result of his listening the eunuch got saved. **(Read Acts**

**10:19-21 & v.44-45)** Praise God! Not only did they get saved, they were filled with the Holy Ghost. You know they were saved because Jesus doesn't baptize sinners in the Holy Ghost, you must be a believer.

When you are witnessing don't do all of the talking. Some believers never let the sinner say anything. There is more to being a good witness than just knowing the Bible. You must also have the skill of being a good listener.

If you are interested in what they are saying then they might be interested in what you have to say. People like it when someone is interested in them. They feel good about themselves and have more self-esteem. Their heart is being prepared to receive the Word of God.

This is the time that you need to witness and they need to listen to you. Remember in the Parable of the Sower, you need good ground which is their heart. Be led by the Holy Spirit and begin to witness. Let the Holy Spirit work through you. He does the convicting and draws them to Jesus.

If you don't listen to them and show an interest in them they won't always be open to what you are saying. Think about it. When people talk to you, do you want them to listen and be interested in you? Of course, you do. Now think about how the sinner feels when a Christian tells them Jesus loves them but His followers won't listen to the need of the sinner. Sometimes people just need to get things off their chest and open up to somebody. **(Read Matthew 5:44-45)**

# CHAPTER 14

# THE ROLE OF THE HOLY SPIRIT

In most scriptures witness means to testify. It is a person who can give the details of what they see or hear. The apostles are the original witnesses to testify about Jesus being raised from the dead because He appeared to them and they were His followers. The Holy Spirit and apostles testify of Jesus. **(Read John 15:26-27 cf. Acts 5:32)**

In the book of Acts it records how time after time the apostles and others gave witness to Jesus. Peter gave a sermon on the day of Pentecost and then again when the lame man was healed. As a result of his preaching 8,000 got saved. Peter gave a witness for Jesus by allowing the Holy Spirit to flow through him.

We are all familiar with **Acts 1:8** which says **But ye shall receive power, AFTER the Holy Ghost is come upon you and ye shall be WITNESSES unto Me both in Jerusalem, and in all Judea, and in Samaria, and unto the uttermost part of the earth.**

The Holy Spirit changed the lives of everybody that was in the upper room that day. He took the apostles and turned them into leaders of the early church. These are the same men who forsook Jesus just weeks before

Pentecost. The Holy Spirit used them for preaching, miracles, signs and wonders, casting out devils, raising the dead, etc.

If you want to be a good witness for our Lord like the apostles then you need to receive the baptism of the Holy Ghost. And let Him do a work in your life and flow through you the same way He did the apostles. There is more to the anointing than receiving gifts of the Spirit, even though they are important. The Holy Spirit gives you the ability, boldness, strength and wisdom to testify for Jesus. (Read about Stephen's sermon in **Acts 7** for a good example of this)

Peter preached without the gifts of the Spirit being manifested when the lame man was healed that was a manifestation of a gift of the Spirit. But DURING Peter's sermon the gifts of the Spirit were not manifested. Why? The gifts of the Spirit will never replace God's Word. And God's Word will never replace the gifts of the Spirit. They work together and never contradict each other.

The Father, Son and Holy Ghost are in agreement and in perfect unity at all times. You will never hear one of them contradict or interrupt another. If the Father has a message through preaching or teaching it happens through the Word. When Jesus has a message for His church, the Holy Spirit will use prophecy or a combination of tongues followed with an interpretation and maybe the word of wisdom. **(Read John 16:13)**

Don't limit what the Holy Spirit can do in your life by thinking all witnessing is done with the gifts of the Spirit. And don't limit Him by thinking all witnessing is done without the gifts of the Spirit. He is not limited to gifts only, but He doesn't want the gifts to be neglected either. **(Read John 16:7-11)**

The parable of the sower is a perfect example of how this works. **(Read Matt. 13:18-23)**

The phrase "by the way side" means when a sinner hears the gospel they are right beside the road that Jesus said was narrow and leads to eternal life. They are right on the shoulder of the road. Then the devil snatched the word that was sown in his heart. Why? Because of sowing and reaping. If God's Word is sown in a sinner's heart then the Holy Spirit can do a work in the sinner's life and continue to deal with them. In verse 19 the sinner rejected Jesus.

I bet people wonder how the devil snatches the word from the sinner. Unbelief will rob sinners of salvation. I can tell you how he tried to do it to me the day I got saved. He tried to convince me that I could get saved some other time. Before I had time to consider what he said, Jesus told me "Today is the day". I went to the altar and got saved. That was the greatest day of my life because that is the day I met my Lord and Savior Jesus Christ. This is what happens when a sinner accepts Jesus into their heart. **(Read Acts 2:37-38** for example)

The Holy Spirit deals with sinners about Jesus being the Son of God, crucified, buried, resurrected and seated at the right hand of God. He deals with them about their need of a Savior and about being lost in sin. He also lets people know that Satan was defeated at Calvary.

Jesus is Lord

The Holy Spirit helps us to say "Jesus is Lord" **(Read 1 Cor. 12:3)**

How do we get saved? **(Read Romans 10:9-10)**

The Holy Spirit exposes deception (false teaching, preaching, prophecy, etc.) **(Read 1 John 4:1-6)**

# CHAPTER 15

# DON'T LIMIT YOURSELF

Don't limit yourself by wasting time on sinners who are stubborn, refuse to listen, want to argue or debate. If they want to resist the faith or come against you then you need to move on to the next sinner who might listen to you. Don't limit yourself to certain places. Witness to all races, rich or poor, gay or straight or anybody else. (**Read 1 Cor. 9:19-23**)

Don't limit yourself by witnessing to only one race. If you do this you can't spread the gospel to other races and colors. If you witness to men only, who will tell the women about Jesus? If you witness to women only, who will tell the men about Jesus? If you witness to adults only, who will tell the children about Jesus? If you witness to children only, who will tell the adults about Jesus? (**Read Mark 16:15**)

I want you to consider the people you witness to. Do you witness to certain people? Do you witness to your family and nobody else? Do you witness to your friends and nobody else? Classmates? Co-workers? Boss? Employees? Etc. Red, yellow, black or white they are ALL precious in His sight.

Witness with tracts. Witness without tracts. Some believers will only witness one way. By doing this you are placing limits on who you can reach. Take yourself out of the box, so to speak and allow God to use you in ways He has never done before. This goes for preaching, teaching, praying, etc. it's not just for witnessing. Don't limit yourself in your preaching or whatever God has called you to do. Pray about it. Live up to your full potential by being humble, obedient, anointed and crucify the flesh. Ask God "Help me to witness (fill in the blank of your calling here) the way You want me to witness".

Prayer

Don't put limits on what God can do in your life by the way you pray. You have not because you ask not. Learn how to pray with a purpose so that you will receive what you pray for. Don't pray empty, meaningless, pointless and aimless prayers that won't accomplish anything for the kingdom of God. Pray for the kingdom of God and His righteousness to be fulfilled. **(Read Matt. 6:33)** Pray for good works to be manifested so God will be glorified. **(Read Matt. 5:16)**

Anointing

We are limited by doing things our way instead of God's way. You cannot win a spiritual battle in the flesh. **(Read Isaiah 55:6-9 and Zech. 4:6)** When we are in the flesh we are limited in how the Holy Spirit can use us. You must be in the Spirit to operate in the gifts of the Spirit. In **1 Cor. 12**, Paul calls them **"spiritual gifts".** The more spiritual you are the more the Holy Spirit will manifest the gifts of the Spirit in you.

The anointing is the power of God. You need the anointing to overcome the power of the devil. We can't forget that this is spiritual warfare. Soul winning is very important.

It is foolish to try to win souls without the anointing. In **Acts 1:8, Jesus said "You shall receive power after the Holy Ghost is come upon you".**

Faith

We hope that sinners will get saved. You need to have faith in soul winning to be successful. When you are praying you need to believe that souls will be saved. **(Read Heb. 11:1 and Mark 11:24)**

Notice Jesus said **"when you pray"**, is the time you need to have faith. Expect souls to be saved. When you got saved or healed you expected it to happen. You believed and had faith to receive. The same thing applies to soul winning. Believe that the Holy Spirit will draw people to Jesus. Our job is to pray and witness. Allow the Holy Spirit to do the rest. Then it is up to the sinner to choose to accept Jesus as Lord and Savior or reject Him.

**Be careful for nothing: but in every thing by prayer and supplication WITH THANKSGIVING let your requests be made known unto God. (Phil. 4:6)**

ALWAYS thank Jesus for saving people BEFORE it happens. Praise is the language of faith.

# CHAPTER 16

# DISCIPLESHIP: SHOW THEM THE WAY!

Many people who say the sinners prayer will often go back into the world if nobody disciples them. There are many backsliders today because the church failed to follow up with the new converts. It is our responsibility to not only win them to Jesus but to show them the way. **(Read Matt. 28:18-20)**

Here are the 5 things the new convert needs to know:

#1 How to pray **(Read Matthew 6:9-13)**

Now let me break down each verse:

**v.9 "Our Father"** means God is our Father and He loves us and cares about our problems as a parent cares for their child but His love for us is much greater. Scripture says He numbered the hairs on our head. **(Read Matthew 10:30)**

**"Hallowed be Thy name"** means God is holy. It is God's nature and character to be holy.

**v.10** God wants us to put His kingdom first. Our earthly desires should take a backseat to what God wants us to do.

**v.11** Jesus said **"I am the Bread of Life".** Jesus said it best when He said **"Man shall not live by bread alone, but by every word that proceeds out of the mouth of God".** (Matthew 4:4)

We need to rely on God for our spiritual manna every day. Israel had to get "fresh or new" manna daily to be fed in the wilderness or they would die. If we don't seek God daily for spiritual manna then we too might perish. Jesus was also letting us know that us depending on God continually is far more important than our earthly needs. You know what happens when you try to eat yesterday's bread. It's not as good as it was before, it's stale. We should seek God daily in prayer, Bible study, praise and obedience. These are the four things that are essential to becoming a strong believer. If you are weak in the Lord examine your life and see which of these four you are lacking.

**v.12** Pardon our trespass and we won't hold a grudge or have resentment to those who have trespassed against us.

**v.13** To be tested with adversity "temptation" and "deliver" means to rescue and draw out of danger or calamity.

#2 Study the Bible **(Read John 17:17)**

#3 Go to church **(Read Hebrews 10:25)**

I like what I heard on the radio recently. "You can watch a ballgame on TV but you don't have the same excitement as being there in person". If you don't go to church then you are missing out on the excitement and blessings from being there. Praise and worship as a group of believers is one of my personal favorite parts of the service. I love when we, as a body of believers can come together and express our love to the Lord through praise, worship and thanksgiving. It's not the same as when you do it alone.

#4 Repentance **(Read Matthew 3:8)**

#5 Baptism in water **(Read Mark 16:16)**

# CHAPTER 17

# DON'T BE PUSHY

One big mistake that believers make is trying to force someone to hear the gospel. If they tell you they aren't interested then don't be pushy and continue to witness. The best thing to do is just leave them alone and move on to the next person. You could say a prayer (under your breath) for that person that the work of the Holy Spirit will be completed. The Holy Spirit can get more done in their life than we can. **(Read Joshua 24:5)**

God gave us will power and choice. Jesus never forced His ministry on anybody. Try to find one time in the gospels where somebody refused to listen to Jesus and He forced Himself on them. There were times when He rebuked people but He never forced anybody to follow Him. Salvation is an open invitation for whosoever calls on Him. **(Read John 13:16)**

Jesus didn't force the kingdom of God on others so why does the church think we can do it? Preaching or witnessing is not being pushy. Even if you are passing out tracts about salvation you aren't doing anything wrong but some people think you are. Recently, I was passing out tracts at a ballgame. Two men made it clear they didn't want one. They weren't rude or anything like that. So I respected their request and didn't give them a tract. If they go to hell I am innocent of their souls because they rejected the gospel that I was trying to give them. **(Read Acts 13:44-46)**

*Jeff Bravard*

The Jews rejected Jesus during His ministry before He died on the cross for them. And here they continue to reject Him by not accepting the gospel that Paul and Barnabas were preaching unto them. Paul and Barnabas didn't waste any time. They immediately turned to the Gentiles to give them the gospel of Jesus Christ. **(Read Matthew 10:11-15)**

In verse 1 Jesus gave the power to heal and power against devils. Then in verse 8, He commands us to **"heal the sick, cleanse the lepers, raise the dead and cast out devils".** The church needs to demonstrate these things by the power of the Holy Ghost. Those who go house to house need to obey verse 8 to be effective in witnessing.

I think 4 of the best gifts of the Spirit to have in witnessing are: **faith** for healing the sick and casting out devils, **discerning of spirits** to know if a devil is present and needs to be cast out and the **word of knowledge** to reveal who needs to be healed and other important facts and the word of wisdom for advice.

Can you imagine what would happen if we obeyed that?

# CHAPTER 18

# THE POWER OF OUR WORDS

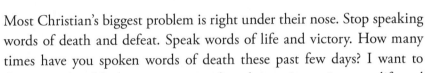

Most Christian's biggest problem is right under their nose. Stop speaking words of death and defeat. Speak words of life and victory. How many times have you spoken words of death these past few days? I want to discuss in detail how to use our words to bring victory into our life and more importantly how to win souls for Christ by learning how to use our words more effectively.

Grievous Words **(Read Prov. 15:1)**

There will be times when you are witnessing and someone will say mean or cruel words to you. The devil is trying to make you angry. So instead of being spiritual you might become carnal. If this happens the Holy Spirit won't be able to use you as much as when you are in the Spirit.

But we need to remember the first part of that proverb which says **"A soft answer turns away wrath"**. Jesus gave us a perfect example while ministering the Sermon on the Mount. **"Love your enemies, bless them that curse you"** (Matt. 5:44) Paul wrote **"Bless them which persecute you: bless, and curse not"**. (Romans 12:4)

Now let's look at the flip side of that. What if you are the person saying cruel words to the sinner? Do you think you will win souls like this? We need to speak the truth but do it with love and understanding. **(Read James 3:2)**

Sometimes we take words very personal and get upset over nothing. The reason we do this is because we aren't walking in love. If we were walking in love we would be more concerned with the needs of others. But there are times when we are just thinking about ourselves. So we get offended over nothing and snap at people in self-defense. What do you think sinners will be thinking when they witness this? **(Read Prov. 10:12 and 10:20)**

Many Words **(Read Prov. 10:19 & 17:28 and Eccl. 5:2)**

I have learned that when I'm witnessing it is actually more effective to speak less than to speak a lot. Instead of you doing all of the talking you want to let the Holy Spirit to flow through you. The Holy Spirit does the convicting not us. When you are silent you can listen to that still, small voice for guidance.

It's not always what you say but how you say it that makes a difference. Notice the difference, I yell at you real loud saying "You need to repent". Then I say it with love and gentleness. I told you the same words but it delivered a different message because of the way I said it.

Jesus taught the people with compassion but when He spoke to the Pharisees, who were hypocrites. He yelled at them and rebuked them because of their hardness of heart. They knew the law of Moses but didn't have a relationship with God.

If Jesus was here in the flesh He would be teaching the sinners about His kingdom with a spirit of love and compassion. He would go to all of the people who the church rejected. The gays & lesbians, those hooked on drugs, alcohol and witchcraft. The poor & needy, homeless, fatherless, prostitutes, drug lords, the sick and oppressed of the devil.

The church turns people away all of the time. Then the same people who turned them away will lift their hands in worship saying "I love you Jesus". As Jesus is sitting on His throne, He looks down on them being disgusted with their behavior. He says "You hypocrites, repent or I will judge you".

If Jesus was here in the flesh He would also be talking to the church leaders like He did the Pharisees in the gospels. He would be pointing out all of the hypocrites. Instead of praising somebody for all the good things they have done. He would explain everything that they are doing wrong and rebuke them sharply. It is the deliberate sin and disobedience that Jesus is disgusted with, not faults and failures.

Words of Life

When you are witnessing you are talking. And when you are talking what are you using to bring them the message? Words! It is important to know what type of words to use when you are witnessing. Different types of words will give you different results. So when you are witnessing you want the end result to be a sinner getting saved. Now you need to know what to say to get what you want. How to use the right words during your conversation to get them converted.

By using the right words you can literally determine how you will impact somebody's life. When God talks to us He doesn't just say anything for the sake of talking to us. He uses words that have a purpose that is in our best interest. Jesus said **"I am come that they might have life and that they might have it more abundantly". (John 10:10) (Read Galatians 5:16-17 and John 6:63-68)**

Pray with a purpose

Pray to accomplish something instead of praying for the sake of praying. For example, I am a soul winner so I devote most of my time for sinners to get saved. I pray for sinners because that is who I am witnessing to. So it makes sense to pray for souls to get saved. To be more specific, I can pray for the sinners that I will be witnessing to that day. **(Read 1 John 5:14-15 and James 2:20)**

It would be foolish for me to pray for souls to be saved and then never witness to them. It would also be foolish to witness to sinners and never pray for them. It is only effective when you pray then witness then pray, etc. Do you see how they flow and work together?

Paul asked the Ephesians to pray for him that utterance may be given to open his mouth boldly and make known the mystery of the gospel. **(Read Eph. 6:19)** If you are a prophet then pray for prophecy to be manifested. If you have a healing ministry then pray for healing to be manifested. **(Read Prov. 10:11)**

If witches throughout the world can speak words against the Body of Christ by saying "sickness, death and poverty". Then the church can speak words to bring healing, long life and prosperity. You can speak words of healing into your body. Jesus told the woman who was bound by a spirit of infirmity **"Woman, thou art loosed from thine infirmity"**. (Read the full text in **Luke 13:10-17**. Also, read the healing of a centurion's servant in **Matthew 8:5-13)**

Peter spoke healing in to the legs of a lame man. **(Read Acts 3:1-10)**

The Lord healed Hezekiah and gave him 15 more years to live. **(Read 2 Kings 20:1-11)** Why? Because Hezekiah prayed about it and God honored his request.

## Complaining **(Read Phil. 2:14-15)**

The Israelites murmured to God in the wilderness so much that they tempted Him. They even asked "Can God provide a table in the wilderness"? Well you know the story how God judged them because of the murmuring. Let that be a lesson to all of us that we should never complain. Never let a sinner hear you complain about anything. It is a terrible way to witness to the lost. Believers are supposed to be victorious and full of joy and giving thanks to God for His mercy and grace. **(Read Psalm 100:4)**

## Control the tongue

A believer who claims to be spiritual and cannot control their tongue deceives their own heart. **(Read James 1:26)** Examine your own life. How often do you lack self-control in your speech? Maybe you get upset and lash out at somebody or do whatever to get even. Whether we like to admit it or not there are some people who just drive us nuts. Look at what James wrote **"let every man be swift to hear, slow to speak, slow to wrath"** **(James 1:19) (Read James 1:20, 3:5-6, 8 & 10 and Prov. 30:32)**

Sin begins in the heart

Have you ever heard somebody say something and then immediately they say "I didn't mean to say that"? Maybe it was foul language, a rude comment or whatever. Did you know it is a sin to refuse to pray or give thanks to God? **(Read 1 Sam. 12:23, 2 Tim. 3:2 & Matt. 12:34) (Read Luke 19:37-40** where Jesus is praised by the multitude.)

I remember when I was in a worship service and the spirit of prophecy fell on me. Then I cried out to God "Lord, You said in Your Word that if we wouldn't praise You the rocks would cry out in our place. I will praise You. I don't want to be replaced by a rock".

Some Christians will never praise and worship the Lord. I mean call on Him with all of your heart and soul and just pour out your love to Him. Tell Him how much you love Him and how thankful you are for every blessing in your life. It truly is an honor and privilege to call on Jesus and be in His presence. I hope we never take that for granted. It is an honor to call God my Father, Jesus my Lord and Savior and the Holy Spirit my Comforter.

# CHAPTER 19

# COMMON QUESTIONS ABOUT GOING TO HEAVEN

This chapter is a tract that I personally made. Just add the verses where I put read then whatever verse it is.

#1 Do good people who aren't Christians go to Heaven? No **(Read Eph. 2:8-9)**

#2 Do all religions lead to Heaven? No **(Read John 14:6 & Acts 4:12)**

#3 Will church membership get me in to Heaven? No **(Read John 3:3)**

#4 Will water baptism alone get me in to Heaven? No **(Read John 3:5)**

#5 Do I have to speak in tongues to go to Heaven? No **(Read Rom. 10:9)**

#6 What do I have to do to go to Heaven? Accept Jesus Christ as your personal Lord and Savior.

Now say this prayer out loud: "Heavenly Father, I believe Jesus is Your Son and You raised Him from the dead. Jesus, forgive me for all of my sins and wash my sins away with Your holy blood. Come into my heart, and be my Lord and Savior. Thank you for saving me. In Jesus name I pray. Amen".

To help you get started in your new life as a Christian. You need to repent of your sins, get baptized in water, start praying and reading the Bible and go to church and tell others that you gave your heart to Jesus.

# CHAPTER 20

# WHY PEOPLE REJECT CHRIST

I don't know who this belongs to but I am including it here because I liked it.

NOT NOW SOME OTHER TIME **(Read Prov. 27:1)**

I AM DOING THE BEST I CAN **(Read Eph. 2:8-9)**

TOO MANY HYPOCRITES **(Read Matt. 7:21)**

ALL ROADS LEAD TO HEAVEN **(Read John 14:6)**

I AM A CHURCH MEMBER **(Read John 3:3)**

GOD WILL NOT CONDEMN ANYONE **(Read John 3:18)**

# CHAPTER 21

# A HEART FOR THE LOST

Having a heart for the lost is what motivates me to win souls. I wouldn't win souls if I didn't care about them. When I am passing out tracts or witnessing one on one. I must sincerely have a concern for them to be a good witness. I try to reach as many people that I possibly can. One question I am always asking myself is "Did I miss anybody"? I don't want to miss one sinner when I'm witnessing. I want everybody to have an opportunity to have a relationship with Jesus. So I try to give everybody a tract. Tracts are a good way to witness. **(Read John 3:16-17)**

God loved us so much that He gave us His best. Jesus was the perfect sacrifice for the world. God didn't send an angel or anybody else to die for our sins. When you love somebody you give or offer them your very best. You must understand how powerful it was for Jesus to leave His throne and become a man. How many kings do you know that would forsake their throne to die for the world?

Jesus came here to save the world not to condemn it. Some people get so confused about why He came. Jesus came to establish the kingdom of God. The biggest need is salvation. Everybody needs to get right with God. That is why John the Baptist preached repentance. Who prepared the way for Jesus. Then Jesus preached about repentance of sins. **(Read Rom. 6:23)**

Imagine a world that is lost and has no hope without Jesus. What if Jesus didn't come to die for us? What if He just stayed in heaven? We would all die and go to hell being lost. God's gift to us is eternal life through Jesus as our personal Lord and Savior. **(Read Rom. 8:31-32)**

Good deeds **(Read Matt. 25:31-46)**

The Body of Christ is responsible for more than just preaching. We need to take care of the poor & needy, widows, orphans, sick, etc. There are many people who have a ministry for such things as feeding the hungry, clothing the naked, giving medicine to those that are sick, visiting people in prison and hospitals, etc. These are just some of the things the Body of Christ is doing to be a blessing to others. The ministry of helps is one of the most important things to do today.

I encourage you to pray about which ministry to support in finances and prayer. While you are praying ask the Lord what else you can do to be a blessing to others. He might want you to start your own ministry of helps or something else. Pray and find out what God has planned for you.

These good deeds reach many people and it touches their hearts to know that someone cares about them. Then when they are touched this allows the perfect opportunity to witness about Jesus dying on the cross for them. There are several people on Christian TV who do a wonderful work for the Lord in helping others. Everybody will be rewarded according to their own labor. **(Read 1 Cor. 3:8)**

I have been having a burden for teens who aren't loved by anybody. They go to school and nobody cares about them there. Then they go home and get ignored by their parents and don't get loved at home either. And we wonder why teens are behaving the way they do these days.

Love is a need. Everybody needs to be loved by somebody. It doesn't matter if you are young or old, you need to be loved by somebody. These teens are crying out for love, attention and affection. Many of them might not admit it but that is the reason some of them get in trouble.

I wish parents would hug their children and tell them how much they love them. I know many parents will say "Oh, they know I love them". Maybe they do, then again maybe they don't. You like it when you are loved by somebody. We all like to hear someone close to us say "I love you". It makes us feel good. If we really want to win souls we need to show the world the love of God in our life. If we don't then they might not listen to us. You know adults need love too. Love is for everybody. **(Read 1 John 4:7-8)**

# CHAPTER 22

# GOING FROM HOUSE TO HOUSE

This is one thing the Jehovah's Witnesses do better than any other religion. They are always knocking on somebody's door. I think they are very persistent in their work. I don't agree with their beliefs but I like their zeal in going from house to house each week.

The Body of Christ could learn from that. We need to go from house to house to win souls and invite people to church. When I do this I take tracts with me to pass out and then invite them to church. If nobody is home I leave a tract there.

A good way to do this is to get a local map, even if you are familiar with the area. Then you can highlight each street after you have reached every home on that street. This is much more organized and you can reach more people. Don't forget to visit the nursing homes, apartments, trailer parks and some places have a senior citizen community. **(Read Matt. 10:1 & 5-15)**

We need to pray for the power of God to be manifested as we are witnessing. Pray for souls to be saved, healing and casting out devils. You know it is the will of God to do it because Jesus commanded us to do it in **Mark 16:15-18.**

Part of the Lord's prayer is **"Thy kingdom come. Thy will be done in earth as it is in heaven" (Matt. 6:10)**. Do you think anybody in heaven needs healing? Are there any devils in heaven? If this doesn't happen in heaven then the church shouldn't let it happen here on earth.

We should have a made up mind that we won't allow sickness or demonic bondage to exist in our community or any other place. Be ready to take action against the enemy in the name of Jesus. Prayer is the key to the anointing. When you go in to a spiritual battle you need to arm yourself with the armor of God, Word of God, power of the Holy Ghost, blood of Jesus, the name of Jesus and faith. Then you will be victorious over the enemy because you aren't using your weapons you are using God's.

Instead of going from house to house being unarmed I encourage you to receive the anointing and use it to win souls for Jesus. If you truly want to make a difference in your church and community then you need the power of the Holy Ghost in your life and ministry. Stop being defeated by the enemy because you lack power in your life. **(Read Eph. 6:10-11)**

If you want the power of God you need to be close to God. He is the source of our power so get hooked up to the power source. When we realize we can't win souls on our own and need the Lord to help us then we can get something done.

The early church got off their blessed assurance and preached the gospel, healed the sick and cast out devils. They didn't sit around waiting for God to do something. They were already told what to do and they did it. If you want revival what are YOU willing to do to make it happen? Holy Ghost revival begins with the Holy Ghost. Read the book of Acts how time after time the Holy Ghost did a work through the apostles.

I'm amazed at how many Christians say they want the book of Acts. They want what they had. Then these same believers aren't willing to do what the apostles did. They received the anointing and obeyed the Lord.

Two by two **(Read Mark 6:7 & 12-13)**

This is a good example of what we need to do today. There is no excuse for those who are anointed to not use what God has given them. Jesus sent them in pairs. There are several times that men did a work in pairs. Elijah and Elisha worked together for about 11 years until Elijah was taken up to heaven in a chariot of fire. Peter and John often ministered together. So did Paul and Barnabas. Ask God who you should work with in going from house to house or whatever you are doing. God may decide to send you a partner. Using a partner is just one of the many ways to witness.

Bless the house **(Read Matthew 10:11-13)**

We need to keep in mind that when Jesus sent the disciples out they weren't gone for that day and then came back. The disciples would be gone for about 3 or 4 weeks. So they needed a place to stay. They didn't just stay with anybody they stayed with whoever was deserving and worthy.

Shake off the dust **(Read Luke 9:5)**

This verse makes it clear that the reason we do it is a testimony against them.

The Apostles continued **(Read Acts 2:46-47 & 5:42)**

I like the phrase in verse 47 **"The Lord added to the church daily"**. If the Lord added believers for them He can do it for us too. That verse said "daily", so there is no need for us to waste time during the week. It all began with the early church "continuing" to go from house to house. They were persistent and kept knocking on doors.

The Parable of the Great Banquet **(Read Luke 14:15-24)**

This is very similar to the phrase in **Revelation 19:19** which says **"Blessed are they which are called unto the marriage supper of the Lamb"**. Blessed means to be fully satisfied.

When we are in the presence of the Lord at the Marriage Supper of the Lamb we won't have a care in the world. We will truly be fully satisfied.

Verses 16-17 are a reference to the rapture. The Lord is coming VERY soon for His bride, the church. We are so close to this happening. I believe the angels in heaven are hastening to prepare things for us. Constantly reminding each other "the time is at hand".

We should fully understand that this time in the church and in history is the greatest time to be alive. Millions of saints before us would love to be here for what we are about to witness. There will be a mighty move of God like never before. This will usher in the coming of our Lord.

*The Spirit of the Lord says "Get ready! If you are not ready you need to get ready. This is the most exciting time to be a Christian. Take the gospel message to the lost souls of the entire world. Jesus is coming sooner than you think. Jesus loves the sinners. He died on the cross for them, He doesn't want any of them to be left behind during the rapture. Know this, the time is at hand for the coming of your Lord. He is coming soon, yes, He is coming.*

*Set your house in order as if you are going away for a vacation. Very soon you will be leaving, you will be taking a trip. You will be caught up in the rapture. Set your house in order by repenting of your sins. Then you will have joy when you see your Lord face to face. But if you refuse to repent of your sins. Then when you see the Lord face to face. He won't be coming to you in mercy. He will be coming to you in judgment. Again, I say unto you, Set your house in order, for your Lord is coming soon".*

Verses 18-20 are very interesting because if you don't know the Greek translation of the phrase "to make excuse". You won't fully understand what is happening here. The greek word is "paraiteomai" which means to beg off, deprecate, decline, shun, avoid, make excuse, intreat, refuse and reject.

I am sure you talked to people before and they would give you an excuse about why they can't be a Christian. But it is totally different for them to simply "refuse" to become a Christian. This is what Jesus is saying here. People are refusing to become a Christian because they feel that there are other things in their life that are much more important. **(Read Luke 14:26)**

The word hate means to love less. Jesus doesn't want us hating others. We are commanded to love one another. There are people who won't serve the Lord because of relationships they have with other people. Some of them refuse to give up certain things in their life to be a Christian.

Jesus is not saying for us to stop loving our family and friends. He is saying that He wants us to put Him first in our life. So He will mean more to us than anybody or anything. Imagine how many people are in hell today because they refused to give up something or someone. **(Read Exodus 20:3, Matthew 22:37-40 & Matthew 16:26)**

When we share our faith we should never ignore or neglect anybody in need of salvation. The handicapped, sick, crippled and poor all need to hear the gospel of Jesus Christ. **"Streets and lanes"** refer both great places and places that are full of poverty, sickness, disease, demonic oppression and violence. These are the places most Christians try to avoid. They may even say "those people are full of the devil". That is why we need to go to them in the power of the Holy Ghost and preach the gospel. **(Read Isaiah 61:1)**

**"Highways"** refer to places that are busy, where people are constantly coming and going as they please. **"Hedges"** refer to places such as nursing homes and prison, where people can't come and go as they please. They are unable to come to us. So it is our duty and responsibility to go to them. **"Compel them to come in"**. Compel means to be persistent in asking, to persuade by reasoning.

People who reject salvation through Christ will also be rejected by Christ. There will be people who will wait too late to call on Jesus. **(Read Genesis 6:3)** The Hebrew meaning for "strive" is to rule, to judge (as umpire), to strive (as at law), to contend and plead with. If the Holy Spirit pulls on a sinners heart. He isn't required to do it again. **(Read Luke 13:22-30)**

# CHAPTER 23

# LOVE

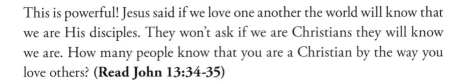

This is powerful! Jesus said if we love one another the world will know that we are His disciples. They won't ask if we are Christians they will know we are. How many people know that you are a Christian by the way you love others? **(Read John 13:34-35)**

It doesn't matter how much you speak in tongues, preach or prophesy. Without love it means nothing. It doesn't matter if you have all nine gifts of the Spirit either. If you don't love others it means nothing. **(Read 1 Cor. 13)**

I hate it when Christians argue or fight especially in a public place where sinners could witness this happening. **(Read Rom. 12:8)** Apostle Paul instructed believers to work out their problems. They were going to court over all kinds of issues. These things were being judged by the world. **(Read 1 Cor. 6:1-7 and Matt. 18:15-20)**

When another Christian sins against us we need to go to that person in private and deal with the issue. Many times it is just a misunderstanding and we make a big deal out of nothing. You can settle the matter and move on. It is best to go to that person immediately. The sooner the situation is addressed and taken care of the better it will be for everyone involved.

Verse 16 is a good way to help settle differences without bringing it to the attention of the entire church. Not all matters should be brought to the congregation. Some of them are dealt with in private as already mentioned.

Jethro gave Moses some wonderful advice, a word of wisdom, regarding how Moses was judging Israel. He warned him that this would wear Moses and the people out. **(Read Exodus 18:17-18)** And they judged the people at all seasons: the hard causes they brought unto Moses, but every small matter they judged themselves. **(Read Exodus 18:26)**

Under the law of Moses, they just took them to the edge of town and stoned them to purge the evil from among them. Imagine what would happen to church membership if pastors everywhere announced we are returning to this same thing. I can already picture people pointing fingers and blaming somebody for something. And they will be the first ones ready to throw stones.

I like the Amplified version of **Matthew 18:18**

**Truly I tell you, whatever you forbid and declare to be improper and unlawful on earth must be what is already forbidden in heaven, and whatever you permit and declare proper and lawful on earth must be what is already permitted in heaven. (Read Phil. 2:14-15)**

I like what Paul is teaching here. When we are disputing with each other the world may find an occasion to use it against us. We should be without reproach, blameless before the world and church. Nobody should be able to name one sin against us. We need to be just like Jesus and follow His example of how to live through adversity. **(Read John 8:46 & 14:30)**

Weak in the faith

Believers should always help one another when we can. Support each other with love and prayer if a brother or sister is weak in the faith. We need to help them by edifying and encouraging them in the faith. Sometimes the church may give up on someone when they need to be praying for that person to grow in the faith and be strong in the Lord. **(Read Galatians 6:1-2 & 10)**

Have a Christ-like attitude

It is easy to hold on to a grudge when we don't walk in the Spirit or in love. I wonder how many Christians today are still holding on to a grudge against another brother or sister in Christ. Maybe it is something that happened a few weeks ago, or a few months ago or even longer. Some people refuse to forgive others and then they wonder why they never get blessed by God. **(Read Luke 17:3-4, James 1:20 and 1 John 4:20)**

CHAPTER 24

# JOY

───────────────

**"the joy of the Lord is your strength" (Nehemiah 8:10)**

Let's face it, sinners won't listen to us if we don't have joy in our life. If you are always depressed, upset or whatever why would a sinner listen to you? They might be thinking all Christians are like that, who never smile or have fun. Part of the fruit of the Spirit is joy. We have joy when we walk in the Spirit by spending time with the Lord in prayer, praise and Bible study. **(Read Gal. 5:16-17 & 22-23)** As you are spending time with the Lord more of the fruit of the Spirit will be manifested in us. **(Read Psalm 1:2-3 and John 15:2)** In the book of **Psalms** it says "in thy presence is the fullness of joy".

As we draw closer to the Lord we will notice that we are growing and becoming strong in the Lord. This is when we will have more victory over the flesh, world and devil. As we are victorious we will also have joy. When you win a game or contest, you have joy. How much more joy will you have when you receive a spiritual victory?

One day I went to the store and I was full of joy at the time because I had just spent time with the Lord. I was going inside and a woman in the parking lot stopped me. She looked at me real serious and said "I don't know what you have but I want it". I told her "It's not a what, it's a who, His name is Jesus and all you have to do is ask".

I don't know how some Christians can serve the Lord and never be full of joy. I love serving the Lord. He is so exciting to be with each day. Read time after time in the Bible where the Lord said or did something that was exciting. Why wouldn't you want to spend intimate time with Him?

Maybe some people have been taught that being a Christian is boring. Not all preachers are preaching a victorious gospel. Some of them are preaching "woe is me" messages. And others aren't even preaching. But they have a fine "program" you can be a part of though. I don't understand these people who think "programs" are more important than preaching the Word of God, having a prayer meeting and praising the Lord. You have churches that will bring in a magician, a counselor and a therapist. The only thing missing is a preacher. One who will preach the truth, the full gospel and not just part of it. Someone who can give the same testimony Paul gave "I declared the full counsel of God".

Praise

Praising the Lord is a good way to lift your spirits. Sometimes we get depressed or upset or maybe we simply need to be motivated. When the enemy comes against you, begin to praise the Lord and He will give you the victory. **(Read Psalm 16:11 & 22:3 and Eph. 5:19-20)**

The best reason to praise the Lord is to express your love for Him. Thank Him for His goodness in your life. Pour out your heart to Him and tell Him how much you love Him.

Don't allow yourself to be distracted by others. Close your eyes and just be yourself. **(Read Psalm 100:4)**

How to Praise

Psalm means a set piece of music. In the Old Testament, several instruments were used such as trumpets, harps, etc. **(Read 1 Chronicles 15:28 and 1 Corinthians 14:26)**

Then you have hymns and spiritual songs.

**Moses' Song (Exodus 15:1-18)**

**Miriam's Song (Exodus 15:19-21)**

**Deborah's Song (Judges 5)**

If you pray in tongues and have never praised the Lord in tongues. I encourage you to start doing it today. **(Read 1 Corinthians 14:15)**

The creation praises God

**Four Beasts (Revelation 4:6-9)**

**(Psalm 148 is loaded!)**

Benefits of Joy **(Read Prov. 15:13)**

We see people every day who look sad, angry, bitter, hopeless or whatever. Do you think these people have a merry heart? Teenagers seem like they always have a hopeless look on their face. Not only are they hopeless but they are empty too. You can just tell that about some people. Something is missing in their life. I don't mean just the sinners. I'm talking about the Christians too. Some Christians have an expression on their face like they are mad at everybody. It is sad that a person would hold on to a grudge and never get over what happened to them. How effective do you think that kind of Christian will be winning souls for Jesus? **(Read Prov. 10:28)**

I just mentioned being hopeless. I bet these same people don't have gladness in their life. When you have hope in your life you usually feel good about yourself, smile and rejoice. Whether you laugh, shout for joy, sing or whatever. We all express our joy in different ways. Some people are quiet while others are loud. **(Read Prov. 17:22)**

When we laugh and have joy we feel better. How many times have you been bored or depressed and something happens and you have joy? **(Read Isaiah 12:3)**

Just like in the natural the Old Testament saints would draw water out of the wells to live, survive and quench their thirst. We need to use joy to draw out the blessings of salvation. The well was used to provide water and life. Salvation is given to us to provide life and blessings. **(Read John 7:37-39)**

We receive many blessings through the Holy Spirit. The anointing is very powerful and we should never neglect it. There is more than just one kind of anointing. And the anointing has several purposes. The anointing is not limited to the gifts of the Spirit only. The gifts are a part of it but not all of it. I encourage you to learn everything you can about the anointing.

Prayer is the key to the anointing. When I don't pray very much I can tell I have little or no anointing. But when I devote more time to prayer there is a big difference. If you don't spend very much time in prayer you might not be as victorious as you could be. You may want to consider examining your prayer life. **Pray without ceasing. (1 Thess. 5:17)** Ask the Lord to teach you how to pray with ALL prayer and supplication in the Spirit. **(Read Eph. 6:18 and Romans 14:17)**

Joy in **Romans 14:17** is the Greek word chara which means cheerfulness, delight and be exceeding joyful. Paul was teaching that we need to focus more on spiritual things that pertain to the kingdom of God. Instead of wasting precious time on carnal and worldly things that don't matter because they don't glorify God and they will pass away. They are temporary things and not eternal things such as righteousness, peace and joy in the Holy Ghost. **(Read 2 Cor. 4:18)**

Notice how we have righteousness, peace and joy; **"in the Holy Ghost".** When we are in the Spirit we can have joy. Remember joy is a part of the Holy Spirit's character and nature. The Word of God says "the pleasures of sin for a season". **(Read Heb. 11:25)** Joy in the Holy Ghost is not seasonal. You can enjoy it as much as you want to. **(Read 2 Peter 3:10-13 and Matt. 5:10-12)**

I am sure that most of us have never experienced the persecution that goes on in foreign lands such as being beaten, arrested, tortured or even killed. I have heard of Christians who had their home or church destroyed. There were times when somebody used a bulldozer to knock it down and other times they set it on fire. There have been Christians who have burned to death. God spared the lives of Shadrech, Meshach and Abed-Nego in the burning fiery furnace. **(Read Daniel 3:24-25)**

The apostles were arrested in **Acts 5:17-42.** Look at their reaction to the persecution in **verses 41-42.** Would we rejoice if we were beaten like that and then commanded to stop preaching in the name of Jesus? Or would we cry unto God "Why are they picking on me"? How many Christians would stop preaching? Or how many would deny Jesus and fall from grace because of persecution? It has happened. We shouldn't judge those who quit preaching or fell from grace due to persecution. Let's face it, we don't know what we would say or do until we are in the same situation they were in. What should our attitude be when it comes to persecution? **(Read 1 Peter 4:12-14)**

We sing a song called "Joy Unspeakable". Peter and Paul made references to us focusing on the glory and blessings we have to look forward to when we get to heaven. We need to look beyond our trials and troubles like Paul, **"press toward the mark for the prize of the high calling of God in Christ Jesus".** (Read Phil. 3:14, 1 Peter 1:6-9, Psalm 30:5, Prov. 15:23, Isaiah 29:19 & 61:3 and John 15:11 & 16:22-24)

# CHAPTER 25

# ZEAL

According to Webster zeal means intense enthusiasm. Some Christians have this and others don't. Many times a new convert is on fire for the Lord and ready to take on the world. Then the fire turns into a small spark. Where do you stand in your walk with God today? Do you still get excited when it is time to pray, read the Bible or go to church? Do you love Jesus as much today as the same day He saved your soul? I love what David said about going to worship. **(Read Psalm 122:1)**

I love going to church because I never know what the Lord is going to do. If I stay home I might miss out on a blessing. When you go to church you should always believe God to do something in the service. Pray about it and be specific as possible. **(Read Mark 11:24 & Phil. 4:6)** I ask God for the gifts of the Spirit to be manifested in every service because they are needed in every church service.

Do you still get excited as you are sitting there listening to the sermon? Or are you too busy thinking about other things? Maybe you get bored and just want the sermon to end so you can leave. Every Christian should enjoy going to church **(Read Psalm 84 & 42:1-2 cf. Psalm 63:1)**

You can tell the difference during worship if somebody is on fire for the Lord or not. Some people will lift their hands and pour out their heart to the Lord while others do little or nothing. Some people observe the Christian life and others live it. The next time you are in a worship service don't hold back any of your love for Jesus during praise and worship. **(Read Matthew 22:37)**

The key to hunger for God is your love for Him. When you love somebody you want to spend time with them. Loving the Lord each day will help you to have more of a hunger for Him. When you understand this is a relationship and not religion your hunger will be ignited.

Your prayer life will change. Instead of asking for blessings according to your desires you will be praying for the will of God and His kingdom to be fulfilled. **(Read Matthew 6:33)** You won't read the Bible just for the sake of reading it. You will read it out of love and devotion. You will be eager to learn more about the Lord and His kingdom. **(Read Matthew 5:6)**

The phrase **"do hunger and thirst after righteousness"** is present participle which means it implies continuous or repeated action. So it's not enough to live in the past by thinking or talking about the "good ole days". You must continue to hunger and thirst after righteousness every day by continually seeking the Lord with all of your heart. **(Read Jeremiah 29:12-13)**

If you haven't been filled with righteousness yet examine your life and see if you are hungry for God. When you do this forget about your past. Are you hungry for God today?

You will be filled with righteousness as a result of continuous or repeated hunger for God. **(Read Phil. 3:13-14)**

This is what Paul did to keep his zeal or hunger for God. He was thrown in jail and he continued to have a zeal for God by singing praises in jail. **(Read Acts 16:25)** Our calling should be our motivation each day. If God called you to do something never lose focus of what you need to do. Forget about the past and worldly things that have nothing to do with your calling. Remove every distraction from your life and be dedicated to the Lord. **(Read Hebrews 12:2)**

Looking means to consider attentively. Many people, both sinners and Christians, often say "I don't know how Jesus went through all that He suffered." **Hebrews 12:2** tells us how He did it. He looked beyond the suffering of the cross and kept His mind on the glory in heaven and the countless sinners who would call on Him through out the ages.

When we realize that the suffering in this world cannot be compared with the glory in heaven. Then we will have more zeal than ever before to conquer every enemy in our life, including sin, the world, the devil, the flesh, etc. When you are faced with trials and temptations just think about how great it is going to be in heaven. Do you really want to risk missing all of that because of some weakness in the flesh? Sin is just temporary pleasure. You want to enter in to the joy of the Lord. **(Read Mark 4:19 and 2 Corinthians 12:9-10)**

We should live our life in such a way that sinners want what we have instead of us wanting what they have. It is very important for us to have both joy and zeal. Think of it this way. If you are trying to sell a car. Are you going to present that car being dirty, banged up, needs repair, etc. of course not. You will fix it up, clean it and the works. You want the buyer to be impressed so they will be interested and buy the car. When you are witnessing do you want to present a gospel that is boring or exciting? If you don't get excited about being a Christian then sinners won't either. **(Read 1 Thess. 4:16-18)**

Comfort is translated "exhort". We need to exhort one another every day with these words. This should give us zeal to win souls because we know that Jesus is coming soon because time is running out. Every Christian should be excited to be alive right now. Those of us who are still alive will enjoy being caught up in the air and never face death.

Paul wrote **"we which are alive"** because he must have believed it could have happened in his lifetime. The early church believed this because they preached the gospel to the then known world. I think it is pretty amazing. They didn't have the modern technology and other things we have available to use. Yet they preached the gospel to the world they knew about.

God is not sending Gabriel, Moses or Paul to do this. Jesus Himself is coming back to get us. The more I think about Jesus coming soon, the more excited I get. It could happen today, next week, next month, next year or whenever. Are you ready? If your not then you need to get ready by repenting of all your sins. **(Read 1 John 1:9)**

I know there are people who mock us saying "you have been saying that for decades, He's not coming". We can rest assured, knowing that He is coming soon! There are too many signs that can not be ignored. **(Read Matthew 24 and 2 Peter 3:9-10)**

There are people in the church today who are not as faithful as they used to be. The Lord deals with them to repent. Remember, the scripture says **"not willing that any should perish but that all should come to repentance".** This includes believers too. There are those in the church who desperately need to repent. We should all be zealous to repent when we are dealt with. **(Read Rev. 3:19-20)** Make a sacrifice, it's not your life, it is Christ in you. You should know that the greater the sacrifice you make, the greater the reward you will receive in heaven. **(Read 1 Cor. 6:20 cf. Luke 14:26-33)**

The life you are living has been bought with a price. When we fully understand the price that Jesus paid for us we will gladly surrender our entire life to Him. As we surrender our life to Jesus our whole attitude changes. The way we think, talk and the rest of our life will change forever.

You will want to preach, teach, prophesy or witness more often. It may become like fire shut up in your bones. **(Read Jer. 20:9)** Whenever you see somebody, you will have a burning desire, a passion, to witness to that person. For all you preachers, the way you preach will change. Then the congregation will get on fire too. You won't have to ask God to send revival because you will be having it. And telling others about the great and powerful things the Holy Ghost is doing in your services.

I want you to get ready for the most powerful and greatest move of God we have ever seen before. I believe with all of my heart this will be the greatest move of God since the Day of Pentecost. People are going to get healed and come out of wheel chairs, saved and filled with the Holy Ghost. I don't mean at a church service either. I mean at the store, gas station, restaurant, sporting event, etc. I see a day where we will be in line waiting to pay for something or make a deposit at the bank. The Holy Ghost will move on us to lay hands on somebody to be healed or delivered. He might lead you to win souls as you are in line.

Wealth transfer

Also, get ready for a wealth transfer. When God was getting ready to bring Israel out of Egypt with a mighty hand. He told Moses to tell Israel to borrow from their neighbors, jewels of gold and silver. **(Read Exodus 11:2 & 12:35-36)**

It should be noted that it was customary to give gifts to servants when they departed. Israel had served them for four hundred years. All of those years of hard work while in bondage was being rewarded by God through the Egyptians. **(Read Luke 6:38 & 2 Cor. 9:6)** Read in **Genesis 15:13-14** how God told Abraham what would happen to his seed. Also, read in **Exodus 3:20-22** how God told Moses what was going to happen when God called Moses. **(Read Psalm 105:37)**

CHAPTER 26

# JESUS IS KNOCKING!

There will be times when the Lord will rebuke you. He does this out of love. He loves you so much that He doesn't want to see you miss out on any blessing that could change your life forever. When you are rebuked you need to humble yourself before the Lord and repent. **(Read Psalm 51:17, 1 Peter 5:5-6, 1 Sam. 15:22-23, Rev. 3:19, 1 John 1:7 and Heb. 12:5-6)**

Let the Lord do a work in your life. The Lord is trying to help you to get on the right path He wants you to live. When He sees you going down the path of disobedience He chastises you. Jesus wants you to enjoy having an abundant life. When you are headed in the wrong direction, just like shepherd guides his sheep. Jesus our Good Shepherd will guide us in the right direction.

When we get rebuked we should never harden our heart, get upset or faint. Just accept it and move on. This is how we learn and grow in the Lord. My pastor often says we need to have a teachable spirit. I agree. Without a teachable spirit we won't be willing to listen to correction. In the book of **Proverbs** we are often reminded that we need to listen to correction. **(Read Rev. 3:20 cf. Matt. 7:7-8)**

Think of standing and knocking on a door. Don't you continue to knock if you really want them to answer? Jesus continually knocks on the heart of every Christian. That verse is talking about Christians not sinners. In **verse 14** it says **"unto the angel of Laodiceans"**.

We often use that verse out of context and use it for salvation. It is Jesus calling the church to repentance. The church at Laodicea represents the church of the last days. The city of Laodicea is in ruins today. Look at what Jesus wants us to repent of. **(Read Rev. 3:15-16)**

Lukewarm means lacking enthusiasm. You just read about zeal, which is intense enthusiasm, in the previous chapter. This type of church often compromises their faith and embraces the ways of the world. One way to recognize this kind of church is you will notice they don't have the presence or power of God in their services.

And we wonder why sinners don't get saved when they are in church. That is if you can get them to show up. Some Christians used to be on fire for the Lord. Now they have little or no zeal. They have become lukewarm and need to repent. What is your spiritual temperature: hot, cold or lukewarm? The Holy Spirit already knows! **(Read Rev. 3:17 cf. Eph. 5:25-27)**

What are you doing to lay up treasure in heaven? Are you reaching the lost with the gospel? Are you showing people the love of God? Focus on having eternal prosperity in heaven and not temporary prosperity on earth. **(Read Luke 12:13-21 and Rev. 3:21-22)**

Overcometh means subdue, conquer, prevail and get the victory. **(Read Rev. 2:7, 11, 17, 26-28, 3:5, 12 and 21:7)** We have too much to gain to lose. If there is a sin in your life then repent of it immediately. The Lord loves you and has many blessings for you. The entire Body of Christ needs to get ready for the coming of our Lord. Get everything in your life under the blood of Jesus. I don't know about you but I don't want to miss out on any blessings we just read about in **Revelation.**

In the last days there will be a great falling away. But those who overcome won't have to worry about this. I believe there will be much more deception in this last hour of the church than any other time. The Bible says in the last days there will be Christians who will not endure sound doctrine. They will be deceived because **"they will turn away their ears from the truth, and shall be turned unto fables".** (Read 2 Tim. 4:3-4 cf. 1 Tim. 4:1) We need to get rooted and grounded in the Word of God like never before and don't believe everybody you hear. **(Read John 16:33)**

CHAPTER 27

# THE BLOOD OF JESUS

The blood of Jesus is the one thing that separates Christianity from all other religions in the world. No other religion can claim their sins have been washed away with the blood of Buddha or whoever they believe in and follow. Only the blood of Jesus can wash our sins away. The preacher can't do it, the prophet can't do it and neither can anybody else, only Jesus. That should make us all want to praise Him right now. **(Read Hebrews 9:22)**

It is through the blood of Jesus that we have faith and salvation. **(Read Romans 3:21-31)** I don't know why we don't sing, preach and teach more about our Lord's shed blood. You wouldn't have the Holy Ghost in your life if it wasn't for the blood of Jesus. You wouldn't have any of the blessings that you enjoy if it wasn't for the blood of Jesus.

When you are witnessing to someone from another religion always mention the things that make us different from them. Which is the death, blood and resurrection of Jesus. Also, mention the love of Jesus. Keep your witnessing focused on that and you will be more effective in winning them to Jesus.

Billy Graham was a powerful preacher who won thousands or possibly even millions of people to Christ. He kept the sermons focused on the cross, blood and resurrection of Jesus. He talked about God's love for the sinner. Billy Graham was a man who had an anointing to win souls through preaching the gospel.

Some people have said they want to be just like him. I understand what they mean. They want to win thousands of souls to Christ too. We have to be careful that we don't covet or emulate anybody else. I believe God has a unique anointing and will for each Christian. If God blesses you and me with two different kinds of an anointing. We need to accept what God has given us and use it for His glory. Just because God uses somebody in a different way than He is using you that doesn't mean that they are better or worse. It just means God has a different plan for you. Pray and find out what it is. **(Read Prov. 3:5-6)**

Blood is the life

In the Old Covenant, on the Day of Atonement their sins were covered up with the blood of bulls and goats. In the New Covenant, our sins are washed away by the blood of Jesus. In the Old Covenant, the high priests had to continually make sacrifices for sins. In the New Covenant, Jesus our High Priest **"Entered in ONCE into the holy place, having eternal redemption for us".** (Heb. 9:12 cf. Heb. 9:25-26, Lev. 17:11 and Matt. 26-28)

Communion

Jesus isn't talking about just participating in a ceremony. He wants us to do this in remembrance of Him. **(Read 1 Cor. 11:23-26 and John 6:53-56)** And continually remain in Him by being faithful and obedient to Him and His commandments every day. Communion is for the faithful Christians who truly love the Lord. I don't think it is wise to allow everybody to have communion in the worship service. Unfaithful Christians, backsliders and sinners should not take communion. **(Read 1 Cor. 11:27-30)**

Unworthily means to have a lack of a feeling of deep respect, love and awe; disrespect. These are the people who should not take communion. Also, anyone who has an unconfessed sin that needs to be forgiven. **(Read Matt. 6:14-15 and 1 John 1:9)**

A better sacrifice

I can't even imagine what it must have been like in the Old Testament to constantly sacrifice bulls and goats for their sins. I wonder how many bulls and goats were sacrificed each year. You have to think they had many people. They are the seed of Abraham.

I am still amazed how God took Israel, made them His own people and now they are a nation. They were in Egypt for four hundred years in bondage. God calls Moses to deliver His people out of Egypt. Moses was an old man. It's not like they could just get up and leave whenever they wanted to. **(Read Exodus 12** about the Passover.)

God told Moses to make every household to sacrifice a lamb without blemish which is symbolic of Christ being offered as the Lamb of God, who was without sin. Then in verse 7 they are told to take the blood and strike it on the two side posts and on the upper door post of the houses. The blood is symbolic of the blood of Jesus. In verse 8, them eating the flesh is symbolic of the communion. **(Read John 6:53-54)** Not only does the blood cleanse us from sin but it also provides deliverance. **(Read Heb. 9:13-14, Psalm 103:12 and 2 Cor. 5:17)**

Our life changes when we get saved including our thoughts, we don't think the same way that we used to when we were living in sin. We change our speech too. Maybe some used to curse, lie and gossip then God cleaned you up. You don't want those things in your life any more. You would rather praise, pray or give a testimony.

Our desires even change, we do things now we didn't do when we were lost in sin. Praying, reading the Bible, singing praises to God, witnessing, watching Christian TV, etc. All of those changes happened in our life because of the blood of Jesus. We can't brag about our holiness because God gave it to us.

I like some of the songs about the blood of Jesus:

"There is Power in the Blood", "Nothing But the Blood", "I See a Crimson Stream" & "The Blood That Stained the Old Rugged Cross" **(Read Hebrews 10:4-6)**

God was not pleased with empty and meaningless sacrifices from people who were full of sin. He wants the sacrifices to come from a person who loves and obeys Him.

A person who offers their best sacrifice. The priests were offering the worst bulls and goats they could find.

God wouldn't have rejected their offerings if they were sincere and obedient to His commandments. Not only was the offering rejected, many times so was the high priest. A high priest should be holy before God and man. When Jesus rose from the dead He became our High Priest. **(Read Rom. 5:6-11)**

Verse 6 is saying we were hopeless until Jesus died for us. We were spiritually dead and Jesus gave us life when we got saved. There was nothing we could say or do to help ourselves. **(Read Isaiah 64:6)**

In the Old Testament, the saints relied on the law for salvation. But they weren't always faithful and obedient to the law. **(Read 1 John 3:4)** You can't earn salvation by works, it is the gift of God. **(Read Eph. 2:8-9)** Many people think that being a good person will get them to heaven. They are deceived because that is not true. Jesus is the only way to heaven. **(Read John 14:6 & Acts 4:12)**

We were not worthy of God's love for us. God knew our need of a Savior so He provided one, Jesus. He knew we were going to hell unless some great thing would happen to us. That great thing is Jesus giving His life so we could have eternal life. **(Read John 15:13 and John 3:16)**

We are justified and innocent by the blood of Jesus. We don't have to worry about going to hell. When our sins are washed away it's as if they never happened. **Psalm 136** says over and over **"His mercy endureth forever".** If it wasn't for His mercy we would all be in trouble.

**Romans 5:10** is powerful! When we were enemies God loved us enough to provide salvation through the death of His only begotten Son, Jesus.

We are blessed by the life of Jesus. If Jesus didn't rise from the dead then He wouldn't be able to save our souls. **(Read Romans 8:32)**

Most, if not all Christians put limits or restrictions on what God can do in their life because of their unbelief and disobedience. **(Read James 1:6-7)** Many times we just don't ask God in prayer to do what we want. **(Read James 4:2)** Then we sit around wondering why we aren't blessed. If we aren't careful we may end up blaming God for our situation instead of taking responsibility for our own mistakes.

How do we come boldly to the throne of grace? **(Read Hebrews 4:14-15)**

What is the believer's assurance? **(Read Hebrews 10:22)**

Christians who are faithful can pray with more faith and assurance. They know their sins have been forgiven so they can pray with faith. The believer who is unsure of himself will hide from God by not praying just like Adam and Eve did in the Garden of Eden when they sinned. **(Read Gen. 3:8)**

They hid because of their guilty conscience. They knew they did something they shouldn't have done. So they played hide and seek with God, just like so many Christians do today.

Sin and then hide from God by not praying, going to church or whatever. When we are cleansed by the blood of Jesus we won't have this problem. We need to be cleansed continually. Stop living in the past when you are cleansed. Are you cleansed today?

God seeks us because He loves us. Even though we insist on hiding from Him, He continues to seek us. What else does the Word of God say about "hide and seek"? **(Read Jer. 29:13, Psalm 14:2-3 & 27:8-9)**

# CHAPTER 28

# CROSS

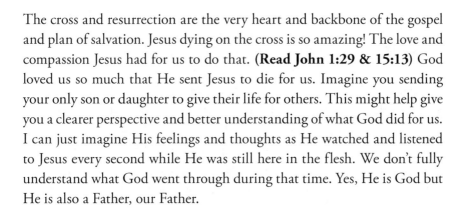

The cross and resurrection are the very heart and backbone of the gospel and plan of salvation. Jesus dying on the cross is so amazing! The love and compassion Jesus had for us to do that. **(Read John 1:29 & 15:13)** God loved us so much that He sent Jesus to die for us. Imagine you sending your only son or daughter to give their life for others. This might help give you a clearer perspective and better understanding of what God did for us. I can just imagine His feelings and thoughts as He watched and listened to Jesus every second while He was still here in the flesh. We don't fully understand what God went through during that time. Yes, He is God but He is also a Father, our Father.

10 Parts of our Lord's Suffering

#### #1 **(Read Luke 22:44)**

Jesus was very emotional because He knew the pain and suffering He was about to go through. It was so intense that Jesus was sweating blood. Can you imagine the agony our Lord was going through? The thoughts that were racing through His mind. And the emotions that gripped His heart. Jesus had so much love and passion for obeying the Father and doing His will. He willfully laid aside His own desires to please the Father by obeying Him in order to finish the work that the Father sent Him to do. **(Read Matthew 26:39)**

#2 **(Read Matthew 26:64-68)**

Every time I read this I get angry and disgusted. I hate knowing that Jesus was treated with such disrespect and hate. Jesus was blindfolded, hit, mocked and they even spit in His face. I wonder what Jesus thought about the people who were doing this. He is full of love and mercy towards all men. We know He forgave them because He asked the Father to forgive them.

#3 **(Read Matthew 27:2)**

Peter denies Jesus. As this is happening Judas hangs himself. Then Jesus is before Pilate where He is accused by the chief priests and says nothing. Pilate marveled at this greatly. Most people who are falsely accused are eager to say something in their own defense. **(Read Acts 8:32)**

#4 **(Read Matthew 27:26 cf. Isaiah 53:5)**

The victims of a Roman flogging would be stripped and stretched against a pillar with their hands tied. Then two Roman soldiers would use wooden handles with leather thongs attached to it. And bones or other objects would be tied or attached to the thongs for a brutal beating. One soldier stands on each side. The two of them would take turns and beat the helpless victim which often resulted in death.

#5 **(Read Matthew 27:28-30)**

They were mocking Him out of ignorance. **(Read Acts 3:13-18)** I honestly don't think all of them understood what was happening or many of them would have repented. They witnessed the miracles and heard Him teach yet many of them rejected Him. Just like they killed the prophets that God sent them. They were doing the same things their fathers did.

I wonder how many of these people repented and gave their heart to the Lord when He rose from the dead. Maybe some of them were in the crowd of the 3,000 who got saved on the Day of Pentecost when Peter delivered a powerful sermon. Or maybe they were among the 5,000 who got saved when the lame man was healed and Peter gave another sermon. You can say whatever you want to about Peter but he is the only preacher I know of who converted about 8,000 sinners during his first two sermons to the lost.

If you want to study more about what happened at Calvary study the entire chapter of **Isaiah 53.**

#6 **(Read Matthew 27:31 and John 19:17)**

I love how Jesus never stopped reaching out to others even as He was going to the cross. Right before He was crucified He was talking to women who were weeping for Him. And Jesus told them **"Daughters of Jerusalem, weep not for Me, but weep for yourselves and for your children"** (Read **Luke 23:26-32** for full text.)

#7 **(Read Matthew 27:35)**

#8 **(Read Luke 23:35-39)**

Jesus suffered so much and then He had to endure the insults of others. They were using His own words to insult or mock Him. They mentioned Him being the King of the Jews for two reasons 1) they rejected Him saying "We have no king but Caesar" **(Read John 19:15)** 2) He said He was King of the Jews. Even the thieves were insulting Him. Actually, I think he was tempting or testing Jesus to see if he could be saved from death or not.

#9 **(Read Matthew 27:46-49)**

Nothing touches my heart more than Jesus crying out "My God, My God, why hast thou forsaken Me"? As bad as the physical suffering was I can't begin to imagine how our Lord suffered as He uttered those powerful words. I wonder what was going through His mind at that moment. And what it must have been like to suffer from having a broken heart.

#10 **(Read Matthew 27:50, Luke 23:46, John 19:30 and 2 Cor. 5:21)**

This is the end of His suffering!

**(Read Matthew 27:51-54 cf. Ephesians 2:13-16)**

The veil of the temple being rent opened the way for us to enter the presence of God. The veil separated the holy and the most holy. Before this only the high priest could enter in to the most holy, the presence of God. Jesus became our High Priest and in His name we can enter in to God's presence whenever we want to.

In the Old Testament the high priest entered in once per year to offer a sacrifice for the people. Jesus offered Himself by dying on the cross and became the perfect sacrifice without blemish, the Lamb of God. God wanted an acceptable sacrifice with no blemish. In Exodus, God told Moses to tell the people to offer a lamb without blemish on Passover. **"Christ our Passover is sacrificed for us" (1 Cor. 5:7)**

I can't even fathom what it must have been like for those people who were there when all of this took place. Just a few hours before this they were mocking Jesus. Now they are full of fear because of the things they just witnessed. I think the graves being opened would have been enough to get my attention. The saints arose and came out of the graves then went to Jerusalem and appeared unto many. **(Read Phil. 2:6-11)**

The Trinity is the Father, Son and Holy Ghost. I don't know why some people get offended because Jesus and the Holy Spirit are equal to God. They are three separate persons who make up one God. The Pharisees and chief priests were outraged because they thought Jesus was committing blasphemy when He called Himself the Son of God. **(cf. Matthew 26:63-65)**

Jesus made the biggest sacrifice and God gave Him a name above every name. Not just any name, the only name whereby we must be saved. I believe with all of my heart that the bigger the sacrifice we make the greater the reward will be in heaven. The disciples gave up everything to follow Jesus. Then Jesus told them they would judge the twelve tribes of Israel. **(Read Matt. 19:27-30)**

Results of the cross

Salvation

Jesus is the only way to heaven because of what He did at Calvary and He fulfilled prophecy too. This is by far the most important thing Jesus did for us. He made the way for us to get saved. Jesus is the way, the ONLY way to the Father. I know many people refuse to believe that. If we could get to heaven without Jesus then He died for nothing. We know that His death wasn't in vain. The rest of the world can't understand why we believe this, it's foolishness to them. **(Read John 14:5-6, Acts 4:12 and 1 Corinthians 1:22-23)**

There are people who will always seek God for the wrong reason. Instead of wanting a close, personal relationship they want something else such as a sign, wisdom, healing, etc. There has always been a crowd more interested in entertainment instead of a personal relationship with Jesus. **(Read Acts 13:38-39 and John 5:39-40)**

You can study the Bible and obey the law as much as you want and still go to hell. You must be born again. **(Read John 3:3)** Salvation is a gift that is received and never earned. **(Read Romans 6:23 and Ephesians 2:8-9)** Go ahead and try to obey the Ten Commandments and never fail. **"Our righteousness are as filthy rags" (Read Isaiah 64:6)** Jesus was teaching that eternal life isn't found in the law of Moses. It is found in Jesus and nobody else. The Jews were used to works and earning blessings. Now Jesus wants to give them salvation and they were still thinking they had to obey the law like in the past. In fact, they even tried to force Christian Gentiles to follow the law and be circumcised. **(Read Acts 15:1,5,10-11 & 20 and Galatians 2:16 cf. Romans 3:21-31)** We are Abraham's seed and receive eternal inheritance. **(Read Galatians 3:7-14)**

The promise that God made to Abraham extends to every born again Christian. From generation to generation until today we still have the promise. **(Read Matthew 1:17)** We need to realize how powerful this is for us Gentiles. These blessings were for the Jews then they were passed on to us. And one of those blessings is the promise of the Holy Spirit. The promise is by faith not by law. **(Read Acts 2:38-39)**

Healing

Just think of what our Lord did for us. As He took those stripes, wounds and bruises. He did it for us to be forgiven and healed. Not just physical healing but our spiritual healing too and to bind our broken hearts. **(cf. Romans 4:25 & 5:1-2)** It is ironic that He died for our broken heart and He died of a broken heart.

Sickness and disease does not have power over the Christian. Not only did Jesus die to become your Lord and Savior. He also died to become your Healer and your Great Physician. Jesus gave us all power and authority over the devil. That includes infirmity and anything else in the body. **(Read Matthew 16:19 & 28:18) "They shall lay hands on the sick, and they shall recover" (Mark 16:18)** If we believe we have power over sickness and disease to pray for others then why do we let the devil defeat us by allowing infirmity in our own body? If it was lust or some other devil we would rebuke it and cast it out. Why do we let the spirit of infirmity to remain in our life? **(Read 2 Cor. 3:17, Luke 13:12 and Ephesians 6:12)**

Deliverance

Sin is what binds us and Jesus came to set us free from the power of sin. No matter where you go you will find people who are bound to sin. We see it every day how people are bound to alcohol, drugs, porn, sexual sin, etc. The world has no power over sin but the Word of God does. **(Read Isaiah 61:1 and John 8:31-36)**

Christians should never be in bondage because of sin in their life. Sin has no power over the Christian. **(Read 1 John 3:8-9)** When you accepted Jesus in to your heart from that moment until now Jesus gave you power to overcome sin. **(Read 1 John 4:4 and Galatians 5:16-17)**

One day I was tempted to sin and the Holy Spirit told me "Sin has no power over you. You don't have to commit that sin if you don't want to".

I was in bondage to sin because I kept giving in to the flesh. I don't know why Christians think that just because they are tempted they have to sin or have already sinned because they were tempted.

When we walk in the Spirit by spending time with God we become victorious over sin. Our flesh wants to sin but the Holy Spirit will lead us to righteousness. As we devote more time to prayer and Bible study we become more spiritual and overcome the flesh. The flesh makes us weak and vulnerable to commit sin. The spirit is willing but the flesh is weak.

Jesus also came to deliver us from Satan. That is why He gave us power and authority over the enemy in His name. And Jesus commanded us to cast out devils too. We don't fully understand how serious it is for a person to be bound by Satan.

Let's look at the results of demons having a person in bondage:

The Gadarene **(Read Luke 8:26-39)**

So we see here the devil made this man lose his mind and be insane or not able to use his mind properly. Then Jesus delivered him and he was in his right mind.

Mute **(Read Matthew 9:32-34)**

Blind & dumb **(Read Matthew 12:22)**

Dumb & deaf **(Read Mark 9:14-29 cf. Mark 7:31-37)**

Bowed together **(Read Luke 13:10-17)**

Divination **(Read Acts 16:16-18)**

CHAPTER 29

# THE EMPTY TOMB

Women visit the tomb **(Read Luke 24:1-8)**
The women return to the disciples **(Read Luke 24:9-12)**
Peter and John visit the tomb **(Read John 20:2-10 & 10:17-18 and Matthew 12:39-40)**

The resurrection story can be summed up with one word, victory. Everything that Jesus said or done wouldn't have mattered if He didn't rise from the dead as He promised. Our religion would be no different than others, people who are following a man who claimed to be sent from God.

Cults all over the world have their beliefs just like we have ours. The main difference is we have a risen Lord and Savior and they don't. The other differences are that Jesus offers us eternal life through salvation in Him, His holy blood washes our sins away and cleanses us from all unrighteousness.

The Holy Spirit is our Comforter. He helps us to serve the Lord. The Holy Spirit draws us to Jesus and without Him we would have never been born again. I like to think of it this way. The day I got saved the Holy Spirit introduced me to Jesus and Jesus to me in order to begin our relationship. "Jesus this is Jeff, Jeff this is Jesus". The Holy Spirit sanctifies us to obey the Lord. **(Read 2 Thess. 2:13)** This is part of the work of the Holy Spirit.

We should respect and honor Him more. He is here with us on earth while God and Jesus are in heaven.

When we accept Jesus as our Lord and Savior, God adopts us into His family and God becomes our Father. We become the children of God. **(Read Romans 8:14-17 and Galatians 4:6)**

Appearances of Jesus

Mary Magdalene **(Read John 20:11-18)**

Mary must have really loved Jesus to be willing to carry Him away. Now think about this. Mary was smaller than Jesus. She would have had a very hard time trying to carry Him. Most women can't carry a man that is bigger than they are. Come to think of it there are many men who can't do it either. I don't know how she had planned on taking Him away but I know this, her heart was in the right place. Maybe she didn't fully understand or believe Jesus would rise from the tomb.

All Jesus had to do was to say Mary and she knew it was Jesus. It wasn't like anybody else saying her name. Jesus said "My sheep know My voice" **(John 10)** I wonder why Mary didn't recognize His voice before. Jesus asked her two questions **"Woman, why weepest thou"**? And then He said **"whom seekest thou"**? I guess that is something to ponder.

There has been much debate over this scripture (verse 17) of why Jesus told Mary "Touch Me not". When Jesus rose from the dead, He became our High Priest. Their custom was that nobody can touch the high priest on the Day of Atonement, including his own family. Jesus was going to the Father on behalf of His sacrifice and present the offering that is acceptable to God. **(cf. Hebrews 9:11 & v. 23-28)**

I want to clear up the misunderstanding about His body. Many people have been taught for years that Mary couldn't touch Jesus because His body wasn't developed yet. Jesus had flesh and bones like us but He is far greater and can do greater things than us with His glorified body. I know you need a scripture for proof. Let's look at when Jesus appeared to Thomas and the other disciples. **(Read John 20:26-27)**

If Jesus didn't have a body of bone and flesh then how did He do everything that He did AFTER the resurrection? In **John 20:7,** Jesus laid a napkin that was about His head, wrapped together in a place by itself. If Jesus didn't have a body then explain how He did that. Jesus ate food and went through walls when He appeared to the disciples. Jesus had a glorified body and when we go to heaven we will too. **(Read Phil 3:21)**

Other women **(Read Matthew 28:9-10)**

These are the women who were with Mary at the tomb. They were returning to the disciples when Jesus appeared unto them. This appearance of Jesus was twofold 1) Jesus wanted to prove that He has risen 2) He needed the women to deliver a message to the disciples letting them know to go to Galilee to see Him.

Two on the road to Emmaus **(Read Luke 24:13-35)**

A furlong is 1/8 of a mile, so this means the actual distance in this scripture would be 7 1/2 miles. This is the account of what happened when Jesus had a conversation with them. They discussed the death of Jesus and how these two thought He was the one to redeem Israel but questioned the resurrection because they hadn't seen Jesus yet. The whole time they had no clue they were talking to Jesus. They heard of what happened to the women earlier that day. How they went to the tomb and didn't find the body of Jesus but had seen a vision of angels which said He was alive.

Peter **(Luke 24:34 cf. 1 Cor. 15:5)**
Disciples (excluding Thomas) **(Luke 24:36-49)**
Disciples w/Thomas **(John 20:24-29)**
7 disciples at Sea of Tiberias **(John 21)**
11 disciples on mountain **(Matthew 28:16-20)**
500 in Galilee **(1 Cor. 15:6)**
James **(1 Cor. 15:7)**
Ascension **(Acts 1:3-11)**
Paul **(1 Cor. 15:8)**

Why the resurrection is important?

Jesus is the Son of God

The resurrection is proof that Jesus is the Son of God. I know there are people who say He never rose from the dead. They think the disciples stole His body. First of all, how were they supposed to get passed the guards and move the big stone from the entrance without getting caught? If Jesus never rose from the dead then where is His body? I mean these people seem to have all the answers and explanations for everything in the life of Jesus and not one of them can produce His body. **(Read Rom. 1:4)**

Power of Christ

Jesus earned His honor and glory by doing what the Father told Him to do. Without Jesus there would be no gospel to preach, no story to tell, no hope and no rejoicing in heaven over sinners getting saved. **(Read Eph. 1:18-23)**

Judgment

There will be a day when all who have sinned will regret it. That day is called Judgment Day. If you don't have sin in your life then you don't have to fear judgment. But for those who do, it won't be pretty. There will be weeping and gnashing of teeth. Secrets will be exposed that day and it will shock many. I think the saddest words on that day will be, "Depart from Me, I never knew you". **(Read Acts 17:30-31 and Rom. 2:16)**

Eternal Inheritance **(Read 1 Peter 1:3-4, Heb. 9:15, Gal. 3:18 & 5:19-21)**

Rapture

One of the things Christians talk about is the rapture. We look forward to that day and it gives us hope, comfort and joy. I am convinced this is the generation that will be caught up in the rapture. I heard a song on the radio about the rapture. I don't know the name of the song but part of it said "I don't need an airplane and a jet will take too long". This is how I believe the rapture will happen. Just like Philip was translated from one place to another by the Holy Spirit. I believe this is what will happen to us. **(Read 1 Thess. 4:13-18 and Acts 8:39-40)**

Redemption

Imagine us living in sin with no hope of redemption. We would be lost forever, wandering around feeling miserable knowing that when we die we are doomed. Glory to God! God raised up Jesus by the Holy Spirit, from the dead and gave us hope for eternal life. We have victory in our life because of the resurrection. **(Read 1 Cor. 15:17 and Rom. 4:24-25 cf. Rom. 6:4)**

Fulfilled scripture **(Read Luke 24:44)**

Promise of the Holy Spirit

The church wouldn't enjoy the gifts of the Spirit without the resurrection. No resurrection, no Comforter. And if we don't have a resurrection or a Comforter then there wouldn't be a church. **(Read John 16:7)**

Jesus makes intercession for us **(Read Romans 8:34 and Hebrews 7:25)**

# CHAPTER 30

# LOST CHURCH MEMBER

We are all familiar with this story about the Prodigal Son. He represents the backslider who abandoned the Father's house. This man followed the ways of the world like Demas did. Except this man repented and came back to the Father's house. Scripture makes no mention of Demas repenting.

The father in this story is full of joy that his son returned to him. He goes all out for his son by giving him the best robe, a ring and shoes. The father even killed a fatted calf to eat and celebrate the homecoming of his lost son. Then his other son comes in from the field and this is the one I want to talk about. **(Read Luke 15:25-32)**

The elder son is like many people who go to church today. They go to church for years and they are content just to be in the Father's house. They know who the Father is because they hear about Him every week. They are there faithfully every week for a long time. There are times they get excited and enjoy just being there.

But like the elder son in this parable, the church goer has no idea they are lost. Not all preachers are preaching salvation. In their church you can get rich and get healed but you can't get saved because they don't preach the cross and tell sinners they need to repent and give their heart to Jesus.

God has children NOT grandchildren. Parents can't get you to heaven, church membership can't, baptism can't, ONLY Jesus can save your soul. Somebody needs to preach the gospel to the sinners who are sitting in the congregation. Tell them about the plan of salvation. Shaking the preacher's hand won't get you into heaven. NO PREACHER or PROPHET can get you into heaven. There is only ONE Savior and His name is the Lord Jesus Christ. I'm sick and tired of hearing preachers say the only way to heaven is by joining THEIR church and getting baptized by them. I think you have to get away from those people and go find a real church that preaches the salvation message.

There are way too many sinners going to church and not getting saved. You need the anointing in church to draw people to Jesus. Let the Holy Spirit do His work in your church and lead sinners to Jesus. I don't understand why some churches won't make an altar call for sinners to get saved. If you refuse to do this you could be in danger of judgment! **(Read Matthew 13:19)**

Here is a poem that I wrote:

The Father's Invitation

My Father has a broken heart
   He knows your pain and sees your tears
Call on Him and let your healing start
   Including your past and all of your fears

He watches you from His throne
   He protects you from day to day
And knows that you can't make it on your own
   He longs for you to come home and stay

   To you the Father says:
"Go to the altar and I'll meet you there
   I want you to humbly kneel
Pour out your heart to Me in prayer
   And soon My loving presence, you shall feel"

# CHAPTER 31

# THE END OF THE WORLD

These are the signs:

1st sign Mass deception **(Read Matthew 24:5 & 11)**

How to discern a false prophet **(Read Matthew 7:15-16)**

Signs and wonders will cause many to be deceived. People are curious about the supernatural. Sometimes people are willing to follow signs and wonders half way across the country or around the world. **(Read 2 Thess. 2:3 & 1 Timothy 4:1-2 cf. 2 Timothy 4:2-4)**

2nd sign Wars and rumors of wars **(Read Matthew 24:6-7)**

Let's look at why nation will rise against nation. This happened in the Old Testament. When Asa ruled Judah, the Holy Spirit gave Azariah a message for Asa, all Judah and Benjamin. He told them God is with them as long as they are with God by seeking Him and not forsaking Him. They were warned if you forsake God then He will forsake you.

Israel went for a long season without the true God and a priest and the law. When they were in trouble they turned to the Lord and He blessed them. However, it wasn't safe or peaceful to travel in those days because of war. God caused other nations to rise up against each other. Not just any nation but pagan and heathen nations who were enemies of God's people. **(Read 2 Chron. 15:1-6)**

Just like in those days I believe God will cause the same thing to happen all over the world. Pay attention to the news and see who is fighting who. Pray about it and see how God's hand is in it. People who say God doesn't like war must be reading some other Bible. In the Old Testament, there were plenty of wars and God told Israel to fight. And I don't mean only to defend themselves either. God told them to destroy ALL of their enemies.

When Jesus comes back He will be leading the saints in another war, Armageddon. This time when Jesus comes to earth He won't be a baby in a manger coming to save the world as Lord and Savior. He will be coming on a horse as King of kings and Lord of lords engaging in war against the world executing judgment. **(Read Revelation 19:11-21)**

3rd sign Famine

God warns Pharaoh of a famine about to come. **(Read Genesis 41 and 2 Kings 8:1)**

4TH sign Pestilences **(Exodus 7-11)**

God sends famine and pestilence as judgment. It is interesting that God used Egypt to spare the lives of many including the children of Israel during a seven year famine. Then 400 years later God nearly destroyed Egypt with plagues to deliver His people and get honor upon Pharaoh. Egypt served many false gods and each plague was directed at a god they served to prove the God of Israel was greater than all gods in Egypt and to build Israel's faith in God.

Ten plagues

#1 The plague of blood **(Exodus 7:14-24 cf. Rev. 16:3-4)**

#2 frogs **(Exodus 8:1-15 cf. Rev. 16:13-14)**

#3 lice **(Exodus 8:16-19)**

#4 flies **(Exodus 8:20-32)**

#5 animals die **(Exodus 9:1-7)**

The bull was a chief god in Egypt, so this was a grievous loss for them and so was the crocodile.

#6 boils **(Exodus 9:8-12)**

#7 hail **(Exodus 9:13-35 cf. Rev. 16:21)**

#8 locusts **(Exodus 10:1-20)**

#9 darkness **(Exodus 10:21-29 cf. Rev. 16:10-11)**

#10 firstborn **(Exodus 11)**

5th sign Earthquakes (as God's judgment) **Numbers 16:28-34 cf. Rev. 6:12, 8:5, 11:13 & 19, 16:18 and Matthew 24:8**

6th sign Persecution verse 9

7th sign Betrayal verse 10

8th sign Great Commission is complete. The entire world hears the gospel. Verse 14 **(Read Matt. 24:14)**

Great Tribulation **(Read Matthew 24:15-31)**

CHAPTER 32

# USING TRACTS TO WITNESS

Why should I use tracts?

You can reach people with tracts that you normally wouldn't be able to witness to. I use tracts and they work. I will give you an example of how I did this. I was passing out tracts one day and there was a group of young boys that I gave tracts to. They all invited Jesus into their heart. Praise God! Some people think it is just a piece of paper. Actually, it is much more than that it is the Word of God which is very powerful! One verse says "My word shall not return unto me void but shall accomplish that which it is sent out to do". **(Read Hebrews 4:12-13)**

How and where to use

Just pass them out to as many as you can. You can give one to a cashier when you go shopping or go to a gas station or go out to eat. When you are leaving a tip you can leave one. Some places don't allow you to do this. You might want to ask first to make sure it's OK. Sometimes I put them on parked cars. Some teens were passing out tracts in the summer, along with bottles of ice cold water. I like that idea!

You can give them away to the poor and needy. This is good at food banks and other similar places that feed the poor and needy. Don't forget the homeless, they need Jesus too! Sometimes I go house to house and pass them out and invite them to church. Do this where you feel safe. I suggest you take somebody with you when going from house to house. If you are not sure about how to do this ask your pastor and pray about it.

Try some of these places: sporting events, NASCAR, festivals, flea markets, swap meets, car shows, boat shows and races, malls, concerts, etc. ALWAYS ask first at these places to make sure you are allowed to do this. This is good for people who lack boldness to speak to sinners or just don't know what to say or how to approach them.

What tracts to use

You want a tract similar to the two tracts I wrote in this book (refer to chapters 19-20). Always focus on salvation!

Here is another one I wrote: (I didn't give it a title)

That if you confess with your mouth, "Jesus is Lord", and believe in your heart that God has raised Him from the dead, you will be saved. (Romans 10:9)

Now say this prayer out loud:

"Heavenly Father, I believe Jesus is Your Son and You raised Him from the dead. Jesus, forgive me for all of my sins and wash my sins away with Your holy blood. Come into my heart, and be my personal Lord and Savior. Thank you for saving me. In Jesus name I pray, Amen".

To help you get started in your new life as a Christian, begin praying and reading the Bible every day and go to church every Sunday.

# CHAPTER 33

# LET THE MASTER CHANGE YOU!

Our Master, the Lord Jesus Christ, loves us and He wants us to love Him with all of our heart. **(Read Matthew 23:37)** If we truly love Him we will do whatever it takes to obey Him. We will be willing to repent of all our sins, worldly ways and surrender our entire life to Him. We should never make excuses about our sinful nature or habits. He wants us to be honest with Him at all times. If we struggle with something then pray about it. Ask the Lord to help you get the victory over that sin or whatever it is that you are going through. It might be a habit that is not necessarily a sin but something you want help with. **(Read 2 Cor. 5:17, Rom. 6:15-16 cf. John 8:34)**

When you walk in the Spirit, the Holy Spirit will help you win the battle that you struggle with and make you stronger. I can honestly say that prayer and Bible study has changed my life. A good way to crucify the flesh is to devote your life to prayer. I don't mean all day every day. When you pray a lot every day you will change. You can't stay in His presence each day and stay the same.

Look at what happened to Moses when he was alone with God all that time. He came down from the mountain and the people noticed a change in him. His face shone and he had to wear a veil around them. That is just like religious people. They never want to see the glory of God. They are more interested in being religious than righteous. **(Read Psalm 119:11 & 1:2)**

Obey the Word **(Read Matthew 7:24-27)**

Bible study **(Read 2 Timothy 2:15 & 3:16-17)**

Worship **(Read John 4:24 and 1 Cor. 14:24-25)**

**"in spirit"** means to live a life directed by the Holy Spirit. **"in truth"** means to be in unity with Christ by obeying Him daily.

Some people don't worship God at church because they are not obeying Him. The ones who truly love Him are the ones lifting their hands in worship and expressing a true heartfelt love for Him. Jesus said "If ye love Me, keep My commandments".

Church

If you stay home from worship services, you are missing a blessing every time the doors are open. That is if you are able to go to church. Some people can't go due to physical problems or they don't have a ride. I know we are the church and the church we go to is the building. But we all need to be around other believers for love, faith, fellowship, edification and exhortation. I don't want to miss a single worship service because I never know what is going to happen. That might be the service that Holy Ghost revival starts. **(Read Hebrews 10:25)**

I must warn you that we are coming into a time that you cannot believe everybody in church. False preachers, false teachers and false prophets shall rise up and deceive MANY. Don't be surprised if you begin seeing signs and wonders. **(cf. Matt. 15:24)** Examine if what they are saying or doing is according to the Bible or not. Also, pray for discerning of spirits. ALWAYS pray about it if you aren't sure. Don't take anybody's word for it you need to seek God's Word.

Total surrender

The Lord wants us to totally surrender our entire life to Him in love, faith and obedience. I already mentioned prayer, Bible study, worship and church. What about repentance and having a made up mind that we are serving Him no matter what happens, regardless of the situation.

Some people walk away from God because the death of a loved one, whether it is family, a friend or whoever. We should never allow these tough times to cause us to lose our faith in God. God loves you more than you know. Too many people blame God during times like this, including Christians. I want you to think about it. Is it really worth losing your soul over the death of someone you love and care about? Of course not! **(Read Matt. 22:37, John 14:15 & 15:14, Matt. 16:26 and Hebrews 10:23)**

CHAPTER 34

# HOW TO TURN YOUR FAULTS AND FAILURES INTO VICTORY

Learn from your mistakes **(Read Phil. 3:13-14)**

This is one of the things that I will mention in prayer from time to time. You may be surprised at how much the Holy Spirit will reveal to you when you ask Him to help you. This is a great way to be strong in the Lord. The more you learn the more you will grow and be fruitful. Jesus said **"ye shall know them by their fruits"**. We too are known by the fruit in our life. When we produce fruit in our life, God purges us in order for us to grow even more. Humans are creatures of habit, so be careful what habits you develop in your life. **(Read Romans 6:17 and Galatians 5:16-17)**

It is foolish for us to continue doing things that we know are wrong or a sin. **Proverbs** is a wonderful book on this subject. **(Read Proverbs 3:7-8 and James 4:17)**

Departing from evil through repentance is a good way to learn from our past mistakes. Not all mistakes are a sin. As we draw closer to God, He will impart wisdom, knowledge and understanding to those who are willing to listen. It is insane to do the same thing over and over expecting different results. **(Read Proverbs 15:5 and Revelation 3:19)**

In **Hebrews 12** it mentions to endure the chastening of the Lord. As a father corrects whom he loves, so our Father in heaven deals with us and offers correction. When we are rebuked and given instruction by the Father we should accept the instruction, advice and counsel that He offers us. God loves us so much that He points us in the right direction that He wants us to follow. He does it for our profit and so we can be partakers of His holiness. **(Read Hebrews 12:10)**

A BIG mistake that people make, both sinners and saints, is living in the past. Re-living the past is foolish because of seven reasons.

#1 IT IS FOOLISH because we CAN'T change the past. No matter what happened we can't change it.

#2 IT IS FOOLISH because it is a waste of time and energy. Don't let your past rob you of your future.

#3 IT IS FOOLISH because we will never be able to go back and re-live what happened. Reminding yourself of it is a terrible idea which is tormenting and leads to depression and possibly a hardened heart toward God and others.

#4 IT IS FOOLISH because God is in the now. If we are looking for the answers to our problems in the past we can forget about it because we won't find it. God's name is I AM. That is what He told Moses. If you need help overcoming the past you need to look to God in the PRESENT, right now in prayer and in His word.

#5 IT IS FOOLISH because it can actually destroy or ruin our thoughts and peace of mind and peace of heart. Satan torments us over this. The Holy Spirit never torments us. He is our Comforter and helps us in a time of need such as this. He convicts us and deals with us but He NEVER, EVER torments us.

#6 IT IS FOOLISH because if it is not dealt with soon it could cause a believer to walk away from God forever and fall from grace. This is a serious matter for those who struggle with it. **(Read 1 John 3:20-22)**

#7 IT IS FOOLISH because it causes lots of anxiety and stress. The Bible tells us to be careful (anxious or full of stress) for nothing but to give it to God in prayer and be filled with peace. **(Read Phil. 4:6-7, 1 Peter 5:7 and 2 Cor. 10:3-6)** Now this stress can lead to health problems. Some people need healing because of their past. All that stress just got to them.

OK now let me show you something about our thoughts and how to recognize where those thoughts are coming from.

"Casting down" means to reject. "Imaginations" refer to thoughts that enter our mind from the flesh. These thoughts will be carnal and of the world, distractions to do something else instead of spending time with God.

Every high thing that exalteth itself AGAINST the knowledge of God is a demon. This will be thoughts that are directly against God, His kingdom and His righteousness such as blasphemy, lies about God, false teaching, etc. These thoughts are intended to lead us astray through deception and hardening the heart.

Adam and Eve are a good example. Satan asked Eve "hath God said"? Eve was led astray because she entertained the thought that Satan put in her mind. And we know the rest of the story how man fell. How did the deception begin? A lie directed against God. Eve was deceived not Adam.

Now look at the cross reference for that verse. **(Read Eph. 6:12)** In **Luke 18:8**, the wicked judge was being nagged by a widow constantly. Look at his reaction in verse 5. Why would it weary him? Because it was a continual thought in his mind. If we aren't careful the thoughts that are always on our mind will make us weary just like this judge. He rejected her coming back by avenging her. Also, we need to say out loud "I plead the blood of Jesus over me". Do this every day.

We need to control our thoughts every day. If we don't then the devil will try to. Don't waste your time thinking about things you cannot change. Focus your thoughts and attention on those things you can change. You can't change your past so forget about it. **(Read Phil. 4:8)**

When we think on these things the end of verse 9 says **"and the God of peace shall be with you"**. The best way to overcome the past is to be like Paul **"reaching forth unto those things which are before"** and **"press toward the mark for the prize of the high calling of God in Christ Jesus" (Phil. 3:13-14)** We need to press on to our future by letting go of the past. The sooner we close the door on our past, the sooner God will open the door to our future. Use your ministry to motivate you daily. Think positive thoughts such as, **"I can do ALL things through Christ which strengtheneth me" (Phil. 4:13) (Read Phil. 4:19, Romans 8:28, 31, 37-39)**

When we realize God gives us victory this will encourage us to face our battles and draw closer to God. If we fail or struggle it is because we are trying to fight the battle on our own. But let God help us and THEN we can get the victory. Give God all the glory for your victory. **(Read Matt. 19:26, Zech. 4:6 and Hebrews 12:2-3)**

No matter what trial you are going through today, don't look back, don't give up and always keep your eyes on Jesus and remember how much He loves you. He died on the cross for YOU! That is how much Jesus loves you. Don't allow your faults and failures to come in between you and Jesus. Instead use them to draw closer than ever before. Jesus understands what you are going through because in Hebrews it says He was tempted in all points like we are yet without sin.

He knows you are going through a tough time right now. He doesn't want you to waver in the faith. Be faithful to the Lord and know that He is always with you through every trial and temptation that comes your way. Just like Jesus endured the cross, He wants you to endure your situation. Be filled with faith as you approach it and believe that victory is attainable. The victory Jesus won on the cross should encourage us to continue pressing on from day to day.

Live one day at a time and do your best every day. We can't change the past so don't look back and don't make an effort to try and change it because it is a waste of time. Don't worry about the future because it's not here yet. **(Read Matthew 6:34)**

Many people who have been disappointed in the past hold on to the disappointment and carry it into the future. Some people who seek a blessing from God and don't receive it when they are prayed for may easily give up the next time they are prayed for. Don't allow this to happen to you. If you missed a blessing in the past then continue seeking the Lord each day until you receive it. It might not happen according to your timing. Be patient, don't waver in faith and let the Lord bless you during His time, not yours. **(Read Prov. 3:5-6 and Heb. 11:6)**

# CHAPTER 35

# BE READY!

Here are three parables about this if you want to read them.

Faithful and Unfaithful Servants **(Read Matthew 24:45-51)**

The Ten Virgins **(Read Matthew 25:1-13)**

The Talents **(Read Matthew 25:14-30)**

Christians should be ready all of the time for the rapture. In the last days there will be a falling away. **(Read 2 Thess. 2:3)** We must guard our heart every day and never harden our heart. **(Read 1 Timothy 4:1-2)**

This is a very dangerous place to be in. If you won't hear the truth and accept it then you are opening yourself up to believe a lie and be deceived by the devil. The Holy Spirit is the Spirit of truth and we need to be sensitive to what He says to us. If we continually reject His voice and refuse to listen and repent then we open ourselves up to possibly entering in to a state of apostasy.

We all know the story about Noah and the ark. He preached repentance to the people for a long time, warning them of judgment. They didn't listen to him. They continued to sin as if it didn't matter. When the flood came they tried to enter the ark but it was too late. There will be a day like this coming soon when the church is raptured out of this world. I wonder how many will regret not repenting of their sins. All those times we told them about the rapture and they just mocked us and continued to sin!

God destroyed Sodom and Gomorrah when they refused to repent. They could have repented but they chose not to. They continued to do things that were wicked in the sight of God. Abraham made intercession for them to help them. Look at what the Lord said to Abraham at the end of his intercession. I will not destroy it for ten's sake. **(Read Genesis 18:32)**

Lot's wife was turned into a pillar of salt when she looked back at Sodom and Gomorrah while God was destroying it. Looked back means to scan, look intently at, to regard with pleasure, favor or care. **(Read Hebrews 10:23)**

Let us examine ourselves daily to see if we are right with God or not. Don't play games with God. Your soul is nothing to play around with. Don't have one foot in the church and the other in the world. I believe the Bible makes it clear that you can lose your salvation. Will you be ready for the rapture?

Israel came out of Egypt but Egypt didn't come out of them. The church was brought out of the world but the world is still in the hearts of some in the church. Some people who are in the church on Sunday may be but their heart is still in the world. Jesus called us out of the world. To be in the world but not of the world. **(Read John 17:15-19, 1 John 2:15-17 and Matthew 13:15 cf. 2 Timothy 4:3-4)**

Notice Jesus said the reason they were dull of hearing was because of their heart being waxed gross which means to harden. So something had to happen to these people in order to have a hardened heart. They were already against Jesus and would not accept His words. The hardness of heart is the issue here.

Some Christians could be dull of hearing and end up like this too. We need to listen to what God is saying to us in this last hour. And never turn a deaf ear to what God is saying to us. We should examine our spiritual life. Do I still pray daily? Do I read the Bible? Do I go to church? Have I repented of my sins? Do I worship the Lord? Do I love Jesus? Do I obey the Word of God? Am I sensitive to the Holy Spirit? **(Read Revelation 2:7, Hebrews 3:12 and 1 Corinthians 11:31 cf. 1 John 1:9)**

# CHAPTER 36

# ALLOW GOD TO ARRANGE THE MEETING

**(Read 1 Kings 19:11-13)**

There are many times that we miss God. Maybe we are in the wrong place and miss His plan for us. Then there is timing. We should never get ahead of God because Jesus said **"Follow Me"**. Sometimes we get it backwards and if we aren't careful we get in trouble. We grow in the Lord and we think that we have all of the answers. And we are so spiritual that nobody can tell us anything.

When the Holy Spirit leads us to say or do something we need to listen and obey Him when He tells us to do something. Don't wait too long and miss the opportunity of a blessing. This is what I mean when I say allow God to arrange the meeting. Any time God arranges something for us and we obey Him, we will be blessed. Then on the other hand you don't want to lag so far behind that you miss. God either.

Time after time throughout the Bible, God arranged meeting after meeting and many people were blessed. Even though we may not realize it there were many times God was at work doing something that we couldn't see or understand at the time. God's ways are much higher than our ways. When we learn to trust Him and take Him at His word we will see how good He is to us.

## Joseph

Joseph being thrown in to a pit and sold instead of being killed. Do you really think it was by chance that those merchants were passing by at that time? You think about it. They could have passed by at any time during that day. If they didn't pass by at that time Joseph could have been killed because his brothers wanted him dead. Luckily, Reuben defended Joseph and was sold instead of being killed. God arranged everything for Joseph to have a gift of interpreting dreams, be sold to an Egyptian ruler, Potiphar, have his own throne with power & authority and spared Israel.

Why did God spare the life of Joseph? And how did he rise to fame, power & authority on a throne in Egypt? The anointing! God always protects His anointed people and the anointing for His name sake.

## Moses

About 400 years later there was a king over Egypt who never knew Joseph. He was evil and wanted to deal shrewdly with the children of Israel because they were great in number and mightier than Egypt. He feared they would join their enemies and fight against them too. So he wanted to make them be slaves. He ordered the Hebrew midwives to kill the male babies and save the female.

The midwives feared God and He blessed them. Pharaoh charged all his people saying **"Every son that is born you shall cast into the river, and every daughter you shall save alive"**. A couple of the house of Levi bare a son and hid him for three months. When she could no longer take care of him she put him in an ark of bulrushes and daubed it with slime and then put it in the river. The daughter of Pharaoh went down to wash herself and saw the ark and sent her maid to get it.

Then Pharaoh's daughter opened it and saw the babe cry. She loved the child and had compassion on him. The child's aunt was near and asked her, **"Shall I go and call to you a nurse of the Hebrew women, that she may nurse the child for you"**? Then Pharaoh's daughter said unto her, **"Take this child away and nurse it for me and I will pay you for it"**.

And the woman took the child and nursed it. When the child grew up, she brought him to Pharaoh's daughter and he became her son. She named him Moses because she drew him out of the water.

The man Moses was spying on an Egyptian smiting a Hebrew, one of his brethren. He looked around to see if anybody was watching. So he killed the Egyptian and buried him in the sand. Then the next day Moses went out and two Hebrew men were fighting. Moses was trying to be a peacemaker. Then one of them asked him, **do you plan on killing me like you did the Egyptian?** Moses was terrified and realized that they knew what he had done and ran away.

Moses fled to Midian, got married and had a son. He kept the flock of Jethro his father in law, the priest of Midian. He led the flock to the backside of the desert and came to the mountain of God at Horeb. Then the angel of the Lord appeared unto him in a flame of fire out of the midst of a bush.

Moses looked and the bush burned with fire but was not consumed. He turned to see this great sight. When the Lord saw that Moses turned to see, God called unto him, and said, **Moses, Moses.** And he said, **Here am I.** God told him, **take your shoes off, your standing on holy ground.**

God called Moses to deliver his people who were in bondage in Egypt. He told Moses His name is I AM. Then God gave power to Moses. Not just any power, it was the anointing, the power of the Holy Ghost. If God calls you to do something He will anoint you to fulfill your calling. If you are appointed by God you will be anointed by God.

Now let's think about this for a minute. Moses was supposed to be killed at his birth but God spared his life. And we must remember that he was born of the tribe of Levi, which is the tribe of priesthood. Then God used Pharaoh's own daughter to spare Moses' life. This is the same wicked man that ordered all male babies of the Hebrews to be killed.

Now you think about what would have happened if that wicked man got what he wanted. There would be no Israel. The seed of Abraham would have been completely wiped out. The men can't live forever and he wanted all males to be killed the day they were born. How would they exist if that came to pass? They wouldn't because it's impossible.

Moses was raised in Pharaoh's palace by Pharaoh's daughter. He was educated, trained and had to be familiar with all of the things that took place there. He stayed there until he was a full grown man. Moses fled Egypt because people wanted to kill him. God arranged for Moses to deliver his people. And he wasn't even supposed to have a life and look at how he turned out.

David

The Lord told Samuel to stop mourning for Saul because he was rejected as king over Israel. He sent Samuel to Jesse to anoint one of his sons as the new king of Israel. The Lord said, **for I have provided me a king among his sons.**

Samuel went to offer a sacrifice unto the Lord and anoint a new king. When he arrived at Bethlehem he looked on Eliab and said, **Surely the Lord's anointed is before him.** But the Lord told Samuel not to look at his countenance or his height for the Lord refuses him. Man looks on the outward appearance but the Lord looks on the heart.

Jesse made seven of his sons to pass before Samuel. And Samuel said unto Jesse, **The Lord hath not chosen these.** Samuel asked Jesse if all his children were here. Jesse told him about the youngest being in the field taking care of the sheep. Samuel said unto Jesse, **Send and fetch him: for we will not sit down til he come here**. David was young, ruddy and of a beautiful countenance. The Lord told Samuel, **Arise, anoint him: for this is he.** And the Spirit of the Lord came upon him from that day forward.

Not long after this the Philistines gathered together their armies to battle against Israel. The Philistines stood on a mountain on the other side: and there was a valley between them. The Philistines had a champion named Goliath who was about nine feet tall. The armor that he wore was so heavy that most men couldn't even pick it up, let alone wear it during a battle.

Goliath said, **I defy the armies of Israel this day, give me a man, that we may fight together.** Israel was afraid of the giant. The three oldest sons of Jesse followed Saul to the battle. The Philistines drew near both morning and evening and presented himself forty days.

Jesse told David to go visit his brothers and take some food and see how they are doing. They were in the valley fighting with the Philistines. When David arrived he came to the army where his brothers were and he saluted them. And as David talked with them, Goliath challenged any man to come fight him. He even said the loser has to be the servants of the winner. He wanted Israel to be the Philistines servants. Because he didn't think Israel could defeat him. All the men of Israel fled and were afraid when they saw the giant. **(Read 1 Samuel 17:26)**

David offers to fight Goliath for Israel and he tells the others. Saul lets him know he's just youth going up against a man of war from his youth. He was saying you don't have a chance against him. David told Saul about how he killed a lion and a bear when they took a lamb out of the flock. He went on to say he caught him by the beard, struck them and they died. David also said, this uncircumcised Philistine shall be as one of them seeing he has defied the armies of the living God. David said, **The Lord delivered me out of the paw of the lion and the paw of the bear, He will also deliver me out of the hand of this Philistine.** Saul told David, **Go and the Lord be with you.**

Saul armed David with his armor, helmet of brass, coat of mail, and sword. David hadn't tested them so he removed them and took his staff in his hand and chose five smooth stones out of the brook. He put them in a shepherd's bag and his sling was in his hand and went out to fight Goliath. Goliath cursed David in the name of his gods. Then said to David, **Come to me and I will give your flesh to the fowls of the air and beasts of the field.**

David told Goliath, **You come to me with a spear and a sword, shield. But I come to you in the name of the Lord. This day the Lord will deliver you into my hand. I will smite you and take your head from**

**you. I will give the carcasses of the host of the Philistines to the fowls of the air. That all the earth may know that there is a God in Israel. And all this assembly shall know that the Lord saveth not with sword and spear: for the battle is the Lord's, and He will give you into our hands.**

David took a stone from his bag and slang it and struck Goliath in his forehead so powerful that the stone actually sunk in his forehead and killed him. Goliath fell down to the ground. The champion has been defeated by a mighty hand of God. Then David ran and stood on Goliath. He took his sword and slew him and cut off his head. When the Philistines saw their champion was dead they fled. David took the Philistines head to Jerusalem. Then David came to Saul with the head in his hand.

This is just another example of what can happen when we allow God to arrange the meeting. How did all of this begin? The Lord told Samuel to anoint a new king over Israel. It wasn't the king they were looking for. While others may have seen David only as a shepherd boy, God saw a king.

These are just three of the many meetings arranged by God. Jesus dying on the cross was arranged by God. The final meeting arranged by God is when we spend eternity in heaven or hell. All of these are arranged by God. Will you allow God to arrange meetings in your life?

# CHAPTER 37

# FINISH THE BATTLE

Pray with a purpose

Too many times when we pray we are wasting time with prayers that are not accomplishing anything at all. What I mean is this. Don't pray about things that don't matter, things that are pointless and never bring God any glory. Pray for the kingdom of God to be established, His righteousness and for God to be glorified. Things like salvation, healing, deliverance, etc. When you pray please take time to ask for sinners to be saved.

In **Luke 18:1** it says **"Men ought always to pray"**. During the Sermon on the Mount, Jesus taught us how to pray. Each thing He taught us had a purpose. Read **Matthew 6:9-13** and notice how everything Jesus said has a purpose in different areas of our life. Our salvation, our daily needs, forgiveness, overcoming temptation and establishing the kingdom of God. Just think about every area of your life and pray about it. Don't limit your prayers by only praying for yourself.

For example, let's say I am praying about health. I like to include everybody when I pray for health. "Father, I pray for all of the sinners and saints in this area to be in good health. Four areas that affect our health are: our diet, exercise, medication and stress. Help us to have wisdom in our diet, exercise regularly, avoid medication that we don't need to take and avoid people, places and things that cause us to have stress. In Jesus name, Amen."

Include the entire Body of Christ in your prayers. For those of you interested in learning how sin affects your health read **3 John 2 and John 5:14.**

Pray in the Spirit (I don't mean tongues)

When you are in the Spirit KEEP PRAYING as the Holy Spirit leads you, don't stop! He is trying to do a work with your prayers. If you are praying about salvation and the Holy Spirit moves on you keep praying about salvation and let Him do a work. He might be using you to tear down a stronghold. When you get a spiritual breakthrough THEN bring all of your requests to God.

The Bible says **"Quench not the Spirit"**. If you don't continue to pray in that direction you are quenching the Spirit. ALWAYS be led by the Holy Spirit in your prayers. **"Not by might, nor by power but by my Spirit saith the Lord." (Zech. 4:6)**

When you are praying about something don't stop praying until you are finished. Pray until you get the victory. If you were on the battlefield in the natural you wouldn't look at your watch and say "It's getting late, I need to go". You would finish the fight and stay to win the battle. You would fight your hardest because your life is on the line.

The same thing happens in prayer. Your spiritual life is on the line. You need to pray you're hardest, with faith and in the Spirit. If you're making intercession, don't stop until you feel the burden lifted and the Lord wants you to. Only God knows what is happening in their life and they may desperately need you're prayer NOW.

Praying God's Word

When you are praying always pray according to God's Word. Find out what the Bible teaches about what you are struggling with and need help praying about and win the victory. The Word of God is our weapon in spiritual warfare. **In Ephesians chapter 6 it says "the sword of the Spirit, which is the Word of God".**

When Jesus was tempted by the devil in the wilderness, what weapon did He use? The Word of God! Jesus always said "It is written". Sometimes I will walk around the house reading the Bible out loud when I am home alone.

When I pray I like to use my Bible. I will be praying about something and the Holy Spirit will remind me of a certain scripture. **(Read John 14:26)** Then I can quote it or open the Bible and turn to it then use it in my prayer. We know we are praying according to the will of God when we use scriptures in our prayers that are used in context. **(Read 1 John 5:14-15 cf. 1 John 3:22 & John 15:7)**

When you are praying using God's Word focus on tearing down strongholds of the enemy. In the physical, if we are fighting a natural enemy in a battle and warfare. We would want to concentrate on what makes them strong and then destroy it. **(Read Matt. 12:29)** There are seven key areas the enemy likes to use against God's people: thoughts, words, our past faults and failures, health, money, pride and our emotions. **(Read 2 Cor. 10:3-4)**

Thoughts **(Read 2 Cor. 10:5-6)**

I won't discuss this one because we already went over this one already. (Read chapter 34 for more on this.)

Words **(Read Prov. 18:21 cf. Matt. 12:37)**

One thing we need to remember about the devil is this. He won't know what our problems are unless we tell him. That is how he uses our words against us in spiritual warfare. I can imagine a believer telling their problems and with sarcasm he replies, "Thank you".

The best advice I can give you is this. Stop talking about your problems! When you pray the best thing to do is pray for others first then pray for yourself last. (unless it's an emergency) Then you won't be so obsessed with your problems. Now you are thinking about the needs of others.

You can be subtle in your prayers. Instead of praying "Lord, I am having trouble with my finances. Can you please help me"? Try this. Pray for the entire Body of Christ without mentioning that you have this same problem. If you are born again then you are included too.

God knows your needs before you pray. Ask for wisdom in your prayers. **(Read James 1:5)**

Our past faults and failures (refer to chapter 34)

The only reason the enemy uses our past against us is to discourage us about our future. Things like; "You will never be a preacher. God can't use you, you sinned too much" or "You will never get out of debt, or healed or married". **(Read Heb. 13:8 and Acts 10:34)**

Health **(Read 3 John 2 cf. Exodus 15:26)**

The devil loves it when a Christian is sick or in pain and needs to be healed. When we need healing then that is less time for sharing the gospel with others. When we are busy taking care of our body, instead of telling sinners about Jesus. That is more opportunity that is missed. Who knows how many souls would get saved if the church was in perfect health. **(Read 1 Cor. 6:19-20)**

Money **(Read Psalm 37:25 and 1 Timothy 6:10)**

The church needs money to spread the gospel to all of the sinners around the world. If we don't have any money then how are we going to bless others? Somebody has to take care of the poor and needy. I'm not saying you have to be rich either. Get out of debt because it is a financial bondage. Be faithful in paying tithes and offerings. Give to the local church and other ministries as the Lord enables and deals with you to do so. We should also use wisdom on how to budget our money.

Pride **(Read Prov. 16:18 & 29:23 and 1 Peter 5:5)**

I don't have much to say about pride. "God resists the proud". If you don't want God to resist you then be humble.

Emotions (**Read 2 Cor. 5:7**)

Emotions come and go like the wind but faith will establish you like a rock that can't be moved. Emotions are like the wind, they change directions. Sometimes we are full of joy, then we might be depressed or have anger. Our life can be an emotional roller coaster with twists, turns, highs and lows. Just like on a roller coaster we may scream for joy or maybe fear. Then there are times we think we can't go on any more and just want it all to come to an end. Maybe you even said "Stop the world, I want to get off". (**Read Phil. 4:6**)

This verse makes it clear that anxiety can keep you from prayer. Look what happens when you pray, verse 7 says you will have the peace of God. We all know that faith and prayer go together. Don't let anxiety be a hindrance to prayer. Use it to motivate you because you know you need God to help you. Jesus said **"without Me ye can do nothing".** (**Read John 15:15 and Matt. 6:25-34**) Fear and faith cannot dwell together. (**Read Mark 4:40**)

Listen to and wait on God

When you pray, listen to God. God hears our prayers but we need to stop talking and listen to what God has to say to us. Instead of being obsessed with our own agenda. When we study the Bible, listen to that small still voice and He will guide us into the truth. One thing we often forget or overlook is the Holy Spirit wants to show us things to come. He will reveal certain information about the future if we allow Him to by surrendering our lives to Him and listen. (**Read John 16:13 cf. John 14:26**)

Let God finish the work that He started in your life. Many people have started doing a work for God but they haven't finished it. In **John 4:34** Jesus said He must finish the Father's work. Then in **John 17:4**, Jesus said **"I have finished the work that You gave Me".** What are YOU doing with the work God has given YOU? If you are trying to finish the work by yourself and on your own you will fail. But if you let God help you then you will prosper.

This is a reminder of what happens when we don't pray. (**Read 1 Peter 5:7-9**)

CHAPTER 38

# WHO'S BLOOD IS ON
# YOUR HANDS?

**(Read Ezekiel 33:8-11)** This is talking about the watchman's duty in the Old Testament. Today, in the New Testament, we are required and responsible for warning the sinners to repent. We need to spread the gospel and warn them about hell. Also, tell them about the Rapture and the Great Tribulation. Let them know what will happen to them if they are left behind. **(Read James 4:17)**

I remember one day when I was at a store. The Holy Spirit was dealing with me to witness to a teenager and I didn't do it. I just sat there in my car. Then I went down the street. The Lord let me know that if she doesn't go to heaven that her blood will be on my hands. I panicked and quickly returned to the store to witness to her but she was gone. Then it hit me. What if she goes to hell because of me? Her blood will be on my hands. All I can do is pray for her now. I may never see her again. **(2 Cor. 5:10)**

The Lord wants us to take this matter very seriously and know there will be judgment for those who refuse to warn the wicked. Is there somebody you won't witness to? If so, their blood could be on your hands. If you don't know what to say to them just hand them a tract about salvation. Tell them to have a nice day and then leave. If they have any questions just answer them the best you can. If you don't know the answer then just tell them you don't know.

Now before you get the wrong idea about what this means, let me explain. If you know you are supposed to give the gospel to someone and you don't or refuse to THEN you are responsible for that person.

When I am passing out tracts I try not to miss anybody. I don't want any of them to go to hell. And I don't want any blood on my hands either. We are entering a time when people won't always listen to us. Some of them will turn to cults. I honestly believe we are about to see things we have never seen before.

Look at it from Jesus' point of view. He died on the cross for them. He doesn't want any of them to perish but for all to come to repentance. How do you think Jesus feels when we refuse to tell others about Him? If we don't spread the gospel to the lost then how are we going to face Jesus? I wonder how many people will just stand there looking down because they will be too ashamed of themselves to look up.

Our Heavenly Father longs to adopt sinners into His family and call them His children and express His love for them. Earthly parents enjoy having their children gathered around them. How much more does our Heavenly Father want BILLIONS of sinners to get saved so He can enjoy spending time with each of them in heaven?

Printed in the United States
by Baker & Taylor Publisher Services